HAUNTED SURRY TO SUFFOLK:

Spooky Locations Along Routes 10 and 460

By
Pamela K. Kinney

DreamPunk Press
Norfolk, VA

ISBN 978-1-963928-28-0
        978-1-963928-29-7 (open dyslexic)
        978-1-963928-30-3 (e-book)

DEDICATION

"The will to disbelieve is the greatest deterrent to wider horizons."
~Hans Holzer

"Grandmother's knee is a wonderful place to learn about the Bible, ghosts, and even Santa Claus, but a mighty poor place to learn about history."
~L.B. Taylor, JR.

I dedicate this book to the counties and cities along Routes 10 and 460 East. Their rich, varied, and exciting histories, from the first settlers to the Revolutionary War to the Civil War and later events, have made this a very haunted area.

I also dedicate the book to two writers no longer with us, Hans Holzer and L. B. Taylor, but whose ghost books I have read and treasured. Hans Holzer's books had opened to me a fascinating way of traveling to other states and countries, and that was how I wanted all my ghost books to be—so others could use them to check out all the sites and ghost stories. As for L.B. Taylor, him writing the first Virginia ghost books I've read since moving to the state in 1985, led the way for me to bring Virginia's spirits alive to the readers here and elsewhere in the world.

ACKNOWLEDGEMENTS

I'd like to thank those who allowed me to do my paranormal investigations at the various historical spots, and to those who let me interview them, too.

Thanks to Mike Williams of Baron's Pub for letting Paranormal World Seekers film there overnight on a cold, rainy January night, and for Mike letting me interview him the November before that. Thanks to Central Virginia Paranormal Research and Investigations for your continued study of the paranormal activity at Bacon's Castle. It upped the ante by presenting facts to what was once only legends about the location.

Thanks to Mark Layne and Carol Smith for filming with me that overnighter at Baron's Pub. And thanks to author Deborah Painter for writing the foreword for this book.

Thanks to my husband, Bill Truesdale, for going with me to these places and having my back in writing this book. Also, thanks for working the cameras during the Baron's Pub investigation.

Thanks to Anubis Press, and to Jacob and Jenny Floyd, for letting me write this last ghost book and publishing it.

Thanks most of all to the history and ghost stories of this southeastern section of Hampton Roads. Without all that, there wouldn't be a ghost book.

TABLE OF CONTENTS

FOREWORD

I do not feel that I get to spend enough time in the counties of Surry or Isle of Wight, or in the city of Suffolk anymore. I am working on projects outside of Virginia for the most part now, but for a decade I worked on many wetland and Federal environmental document projects for this mostly rural area. As an ecologist delineating the wetlands, I learned the individual characters of the streams that flowed through these two counties and the city. Did you know, no two streams are the same? They have slightly different bends and courses, slightly different plant assemblages. Many have wonderful names like Great Swamp in Isle of Wight and my favorite swamp name, Pigeonroost Swamp, is in Surry. That one must have obtained its name from the times during the 18th and 19th centuries when the late lamented passenger pigeons filled the trees where the massive flocks stopped to rest.

Such a name reminds us that the history of Surry County goes back a long time. My work took me to places in Surry County, Isle of Wight County and Suffolk that only hunters and surveyors see. I saw the long defunct gas stations and country stores with their ancient, rusted gas pumps, the old churches, the old fish and crab markets along the Pagan River and the James near Route 10, and the half-collapsed houses and barns deep in the woods along and near Route 460, looking every bit like the scary abandoned house in *The Blair Witch Project*. I worked totally alone, always in the daytime hours, of course, since no one can classify soils in the dark. I did not step very far into the old structures because there was no need to do so for the purpose of the environmental documents I was researching and writing. If there was any need to do any extensive work, this decision was left to the archaeologists and historians who prepared our cultural resources reports for the documents. Besides, the stairs and floors were likely rotted from the inside.

In the presence of these places, I often felt the subtle hint of occupancy. Sometimes the occupants were bats and raccoons. Sometimes they could not be seen but only felt. Living people once worked in the dilapidated gas stations, barns and houses. In the old homesteads they ate meals, tucked their children in bed for the night, planted and harvested crops for the markets, took care of their farm animals, and went off to church and school and sometimes, in the case of the people of Suffolk, to the peanut plants downtown or to the shipyards in nearby Portsmouth. These homes and barns were vital places in their lives. I would find myself wondering where these people are now. Do some still haunt these quiet places? I have heard strange stories from a tour guide at Bacons Castle in Surry, and I have read the account of a very old uninhabited home at Cabin Point, also in Surry, owned by the sister of a young merchant seaman from Norfolk. The sister had intended to restore it as a summer vacation home. The seaman and a friend hitchhiked so that one of them could have a date with a Cabin Point girl. After that they planned a good night's sleep at the old place. They got little sleep at the house because both kept getting the impression that the dark grounds were surrounded by restless horses and men, yet they saw neither men nor horses. One of them reported having a very strange dream encounter with a regretful old lady, who was later found to be connected to Baron von Steuben, a Major General in the Continental Army during the Revolutionary War.

Surry County is a prospering county, as is Isle of Wight and Suffolk. The townhouses and the single-family homes, the strip shopping centers and the industrial parks, are continuing to displace the old family farms and stores. But you will still see large tracts of hardwood forests, farms, trailer parks and ponds. Many homes remain as they were over 100 years ago. The people are proud of their history... and their ghosts. To paraphrase a quote about Africa someone made many years ago, "In Surry County, Suffolk and Isle of Wight, the past has hardly stopped breathing."

Pamela K. Kinney assembles older accounts and yet, brings us all-new information about encounters with the paranormal in this intriguing new book about an area of Virginia usually bypassed by travelers interested in larger population areas to the north and east. May it reside on your bookshelf and provide you and yours with enjoyment.

Deborah Painter
Author of *Forry: The Life of Forrest J. Ackerman* and *The Dog Hero in Film*

INTRODUCTION

"What I'm always trying to do with every book is to recreate the effect of the stories we heard as children in front of campfires and fireplaces - the ghost stories that engaged us."
~Charles Palahniuk

Bacons Castle in the twilight

Most times, when heading down to Virginia Beach, we've taken I-64. But as the highway had more accidents and became loaded with more traffic (especially from Memorial Day to Labor Day), Bill suggested we try Route 460, heading southeast. It gets the driver down to Virginia Beach about the same amount of time as taking I-64, and you get a scenic drive without the rush and bustle of the latter. People used these routes before they constructed interstate highways.

These roads might have been what your parents took when you were young, to get to the beach, the amusement park, or to go camping. Back then, if you passed a haunted spot, you might have seen a ghost. But with the advent of I-64, speeding down the asphalt at 60-70 mph, you might be lucky if you catch a glimpse of the building that the spook haunts through the trees.

Besides, routes like 460 and 10 give you time to breathe, even stop at a café or store selling peanuts and knickknacks. That haunted spot is more accessible, and you would be tempted to stop and take a tour. It may seem slower, but oh, so enjoyable. It feels like you would be taking a step back in time on that vacation with your parents.

Country living. Scenic driving. Small towns. Nothing more than that. But wait a moment, this is an introduction to a book on ghosts. Spirits and monsters are stalking these two routes from Surry to Suffolk.

US 460 enters Sussex County as General Mahone Highway, which is named for William Mahone, the builder of the Norfolk and Petersburg Railroad. Mahone and his wife, Otelia Butler Mahone, were responsible for designating the stations along the railroad, including Disputanta. These stations became the towns and villages seen today on either side of US 460.

The highway intersects Main Street in Waverly and meets the southern end of Main Street in the town of Wakefield. It clips the southern corner of Surry County on its way between Sussex and

Southampton counties. The route passes through the town of Ivor and crosses the Blackwater River into the town of Zuni in Isle of Wight County, where the way follows Windsor Highway. East of Windsor, US 460 veers away from the Norfolk Southern rail line and enters the independent city of Suffolk as Pruden Boulevard, northwest of downtown Suffolk. For its ghostly side, there is a ghost tour around Halloween to what haunts this historic and yet, modern, city.

There is another way down to Suffolk: Route 10. It runs from Route 360 in Richmond, east down to Godwin Boulevard in Suffolk. Once you get past Hopewell and into rural Prince George, you'll follow the route of an old stagecoach road. It continues through Surry and Isle of Wight into an area that features many of the preserved James River plantations. Not only that, but there is farmland, single homes, and lots of woods. It passes through Garysville (south of that is the Flowerdew Hundred Plantation and James River National Wildlife Refuge). The route crosses Upper Chippokes Creek into Surry County, and you will pass Smith's Fort, Chippokes Plantation State Park, Bacon's Castle, and the Old Brick Church.

Keep driving on Route 10 to cross into Isle of Wight County. Signs for Fort Huger, Boykin's Tavern, and Fort Boykin Historic Park let you know they are in the area. Eventually, it splits into the southeast as Route 10 Business, which leads into the historic business district of downtown Smithfield. Having a bite to eat at the Smithfield Ice Cream Parlor is worth the stop.

Not long after that, the route makes its way into Suffolk, proclaimed as the biggest little city. It is the birthplace of Planters' Peanuts as well as its mascot, Mr. Peanut.

Simple, accessible routes to travel on, pass through mostly country and small towns, except for Suffolk – lovely sites, friendly people, and yes, the paranormal. As a reader told me at the Suffolk Mystery Authors Festival back on August 13, 2016, she was happy that I was pursuing to write a book on the areas from Surry to Suffolk and that she felt many writers passed it over or combined it with the Tidewater area or Williamsburg. And she was right; the spot deserves its pound of ectoplasmic flesh as it is as haunted as the rest of the Commonwealth. With Surry being considered part of Jamestown Settlement, to having the oldest building in America still standing, and surviving the Revolutionary War and Civil War, it is no wonder this quiet area is hopping with paranormal activity. Peanuts and cotton aren't the only crops. So, instead of taking I-64 to head to the beach, why don't you mosey down either Route 10 or 460? It doesn't matter which one; the phantoms can't wait to scare you.

ALONG ROUTE 10

SURRY COUNTY

"Ghosts, like ladies, never speak till spoke to."
~Richard Harris Barham

County of Surry Courthouse

Surry County is connected to the Historic Triangle (Jamestown, Williamsburg, and Yorktown) across the James River, crossing the

James to the Surry station by way of the Jamestown-Scotland Ferry. Centrally located between Richmond, the Tri-Cities, and Hampton Roads, one can reach it by driving the scenic Route 10—or if you are coming from the Historic Triangle or I-64, the Jamestown-Scotland Ferry— or by Route 460 South.

When the first English settlers sailed up the James River in 1607, they first landed on the south side of the river, near what is now the town of Claremont. Since then, Jamestown settlers affectionately called the opposite shore of the James River, the "Surrey Side," to honor their homeland. It was alleged that the Jamestown colony was a miniature London, due to being on both sides of the James River, similar to how London lies on the Thames, and the south side of the Thames was in the shire of Surrey. Settlements on the south side of the James River were referred to as "over on the Surrey side". The Virginia Company listed sixteen settlers on the Surry side of the James in May of 1625.

In 1652 and 1653, Nathaniel Bacon patented 1,075 acres in the county. In 1665, Arthur Allen built the house now known as Bacon's Castle, the oldest brick building in America and site of the famous Bacon's Rebellion in 1676.

They kept the name "Surry" when the county was chartered in 1652. The year 2012 marked the 350th anniversary of the establishment of Surry County. Following the American Revolutionary War, Surry County became part of the new Commonwealth of Virginia.

Indigenous tribes under the Powhatan Confederation believed it to be sacred tribal land. It was home to several Native American tribes, and the area flourished with natural resources. In the town of Claremont, there is a monument to the Quiyoughcohonack Indian Tribe, commemorating their meeting with the first settlers before the English settled Jamestown the following week. In 1607, one week before the English settlers chose Jamestown Island as the location to start a new colony, they visited this site and feasted with the local Indians. But a directive from England's King James prohibited them from occupying land inhabited by indigenous people, so they decided to move five miles downriver from Claremont.

The first land patent in Claremont was 200 acres granted to George Harrison in 1621. Arthur Allen purchased the land in 1656, and in 1754, William Allen built the manor house, naming it Claremont Manor in 1793. The name Claremont was generally thought to be in honor of the Royal Residence "Claremont" in the Shire of Surrey, England, the birthplace of Queen Victoria.

In May 1861, Company "D" 10th Virginia Battalion of Heavy Artillery was formed and commanded by Captain William Allen, owner of Claremont Plantation in Surry County. They were sent to Jamestown Island and manned the earthworks that inadvertently covered the ruins of Jamestown settlement, which was by this time thought lost to the ages.

In 1875, William Orgain Allen died and his eldest son, also named William, decided to reside in New York and officially gave up his Claremont holdings. Joseph Franklin Mancha of Delaware bought tracts of the Claremont Manor Estate from the Allen family, from 1879 to 1882, for colonization purposes. Mancha divided the outlying areas into small tracts, generally selling to people from the North and Midwest. Mancha developed the land under the name "Claremont Colony." The town of Claremont became incorporated on January 16, 1886, with the idea of establishing a port city to rival Norfolk. Remnants of the old railroad piers remain as well as many of the old homes and retail buildings.

The Town of Dendron is in Surry County, Virginia, and has a population of approximately 300. Dendron was a company town, built and run by the Surry Lumber Company to house its mills and employees. It was known as Mussel Fork Village until 1896 when they renamed it Dendron, a fitting name derived from the Greek word for trees. The years after 1896 saw rapid growth and expansion for both the company and the town, as more people settled in Dendron, and they built more Company housing. By 1906, Dendron had 1513 people, 298 dwellings, two hotels, eighteen Company stores, and five churches. By 1928, Dendron's population had reached nearly 3,000 people. In addition to those establishments listed above, there was also a post office, two schools, a jail, two banks, two doctors, a skating rink, a movie theater, and a number of non-company-owned businesses, such as a drug store, barbershops, garages, cleaning establishments, a pool room, a restaurant, a bakery, and an ice cream parlor.

The Surry Lumber Company closed on October 27, 1927. As they owned most of the town, they had the legal right to destroy what they held, and from 1928 until 1930, much of Dendron became dismantled. Left without the business, a railroad, water system, and electricity, Dendron experienced a final nightmare in February 1931 when a fire destroyed twenty-one buildings on Main Street.

The Surry Side was home to a converted Native American youth, Chanco, who saved the colonists from imminent annihilation at the hands of the native people in 1622. The county has a monument in his memory at the courthouse.

Prior to the War Between the States, the Surry area held the most significant freemen population. Many of those living in Surry today can trace their roots back to the Jamestown era of the 1600s and their ancestors who were slaves. Although that's not to say there still wasn't slavery in the area, just that they also had many freemen.

During the American Civil War, the Confederate Army had units called the Surry Cavalry and the Surry Light Artillery. The Confederacy considered Surry County's riverfront to be the most defensible section of the James River. They fortified Jamestown Island and Swann's Point. The Union found Surry to be an integral part of their communication between Fort Monroe in Hampton and City Point (later to become Hopewell). They laid an underwater telegraph cable from Jamestown to Swann's Point, continuing it to City Point by land.

In over 350 years of existence, the County of Surry has taken care to guard its history and its rural nature. The Surry County records of land transactions are some of the most comprehensive in the nation. They were spirited away to safe hiding places twice in its history, once to protect them from the British Army in the Revolution, and again to protect them from the Union Army in the American Civil War. Surry has made efforts to preserve and protect these original county records, dating from 1652, and continues to house them in the county courthouse.

Attractions in this area besides the Jamestown-Surry Ferry include Chippokes Plantation State Park, Bacon's Castle, Smith's Fort Plantation, Roger's Store Historic Site, Surry Nuclear Information Center, and environmental Hog Island Wildlife Management Area (seasonal and located at 7938 Hog Island Road.). Regular attractions like Slade's Park (Motorcycles/ATVs), Hampton Roads Vineyard & Winery (in Elberon), College Run Farms (seasonal), and Drewry Farms in Wakefield (seasonal). Besides the public attractions, there are also sixteen privately-owned-and- occupied structures in Surry listed on the National Register of Historic Places.

The local government includes the Surry County Courthouse, the Surry County Historical Society and Museum, along with the Surry branch of the Blackwater Regional Library—the other branches are Claremont and in the nearby city of Smithfield. The Surry County Government offices and Surry County Courthouse are located at the intersection of Virginia Routes 10 and 31, about 4 miles from the Jamestown-Scotland Ferry dock on the south side of the James River.

Places to grab something to eat and go, or dine in, are Edwards Virginia Ham Shoppe, Colonial Farmhouse Restaurant and Tavern, Anna's Pizza and Italian Restaurant, and Hogge Seafood in Elberon. Sadly, as my husband and I had passed it many times—especially after exiting the ferry and heading for home—Surrey House Restaurant is closed indefinitely. We had always wanted to stop there and try it, but we never did.

There are various businesses where one can shop in the town of Surry.

Ferry services became established before 1690 in various locations, and residents used the ferry every day to cross the James River to Jamestown. In 1925, the modern motor ferry between Jamestown and Scotland Wharf opened. Today, there is a pier for the Jamestown/Scotland Ferry on the Surry side. The Virginia Department of Transportation provides this 15-minute free ride across the James River, and it offers a unique view of the land as it travels to the James County side and back to Surry. It's not hard to imagine what the first colonists experienced when they traveled on the same river 400 years ago.

Now turn the page and find that all that history is still active in Surry. The dead are waiting to scare...er, share their stories with you!

BACON'S CASTLE

"I loved ghost stories, creaky staircases, stormy
nights. If it guaranteed nightmares, I read it by
flashlight, after midnight."
~Lisa Gardener

I stopped to take this one sunny day and was shocked
to find two faces in the windows of the old section of
Bacon's Castle—one of them looking like a dog, the
other like a woman.

In 1675, a comet blazed across the night sky,
ominous to the Virginia colonists. They believed
that meant pestilence or war. Afterwards, scores
of passenger pigeons flew over and blocked out
the sun. This went on for days. That spring,
locusts swarmed, devouring all plants and leaves
from every tree. When Thomas Mathews's
plantation overseer, Robert Hen, was found barely

alive in a pool of blood, gasping out, "Doegs! Doegs!" before he died, no one was shocked by that the Indian massacre that followed. The Doegs were an Indian tribe known for attacks on white settlers. They made these attacks in retaliation for settlers killing some Doegs caught stealing pigs and other livestock. This would lead to the violent Bacon's Rebellion, led by Nathanial Bacon.

Since Governor Berkeley didn't seem to be doing anything about the massacre caused by the Doegs, the colonists turned to Bacon about leading a retaliatory attack against the Natives. He agreed and did, just after the tribe attacked his own plantation and killed his overseer. His forces pushed the Pamunkey Indians into Dragon's Swamp, then later murdered 100 Susquehannocks and captured others.

Berkeley, angry at this, sent troops after Bacon and his men to capture them. It took a few weeks before Bacon surrendered, and he was brought before Berkeley. Forgiven when he repented, he escaped and returned with 600 men, capturing Jamestown. He demanded a repeal of harsh Colonial laws and wanted a commission to fight Indians. Berkeley granted both, but when Bacon was out chasing the natives again, Berkeley sent troops out after him. Bacon came back and sacked Jamestown, burning it to the ground. Not long after that, Bacon became seriously ill (he had suffered an attack from malaria in Jamestown) and expired from dysentery on October 26, 1676, in Gloucester, at the young age of twenty-nine. Soon after that, many of his followers were captured and executed by hanging. About mid-

September 1676, several of Bacon's rebel followers seized the brick house of Major Allen in Surry and fortified it. Though known as "Allen's Brick House," it became better known as "Bacon's Castle". Despite popular folklore, Bacon never lived at Bacon's Castle, nor is he even known to have visited it, as he died before his men occupied it.

Historians believe the name "Bacon's Castle" was not used until many years after Bacon's Rebellion. The *Virginia Gazette* used that name when it published several articles about Bacon's Rebellion in 1769. However, they hadn't used the name in the records until 1802.

The building had been known as Allen's Brick House as Arthur Allen had it built in 1665. Arthur Allen first patented land on March 14, 1650. He received 200 acres for the transportation of three servants and Alice Tucker, who either was or would shortly become his wife. Allen was appointed one of the Justices of the Peace for Surry County when it became formed in 1652, but that was the only political office the man held. He was one of the wealthiest men in the county. He might have been one of the merchant-planters common in Tidewater Virginia in the mid-seventeenth century (historians are not sure about this), referred to as "Arthur Allen, merchant" in a deed in 1656. Sadly, Arthur Allen didn't live to enjoy his house but made his will on March 10, 1669, and died about three months later. The place remained in the Allen family until 1843, when it was sold at auction. It was while an archeological exploration was going on they discovered a part of a letter that identified Arthur

Allen as the builder and "the younger son of a gentleman." He had sent his own eight-year-old son back to England "for seven or eight years" for education.

There's a small legend connected to Arthur Allen, that he may have been a Prince of the House of Hanover. The story goes to say that he loved the same woman as his twin did and so, stabbed his twin, escaping to the Colonies under an assumed name to start a new life, building his castle and raising his family. Of course, that's only a legend, with no real proof, and you should take it with a grain of salt.

Private Sidney Lanier of the 2nd Battalion, Macon Volunteers, was stationed at nearby Burwell's Bay from May 1863 to October 1864 with the Confederate signal corps. His brother Clifford and he were devoted friends of the Hankins family, who owned Bacon's Castle at the time. The brothers often visited the estate while on duty at Burwell's Bay. Virginia Hankins rejected Sidney Lanier's proposal of marriage not due to him, but because of the obligation she held towards her motherless younger brothers and sisters. Both remained lifelong friends.

Virginia's brother, James DeWitt Hankins, a law student at the University of Virginia at the outbreak of the war, became a member of the university literary society known as the Jefferson Society. Commissioned on June 22, 1861, as the first lieutenant of artillery, Fourth Regiment, Virginia Militia, he survived the war to become promoted to Captain of the Surry Light Artillery and served through Appomattox. Sadly, he was killed by William Underwood in a duel on October

18, 1866, at the Isle of Wight Courthouse, over insults exchanged between the two men while drinking in a tavern earlier. The tragedy started a long-running feud between the Hankins and Underwood families.

At the request of Virginia Hankins, Sidney Lanier wrote "In Memoriam" for her brother, who had been his friend.

Like many plantations in the South following the Civil War, Bacon's Castle faced the problems of loss of manpower due to the emancipation of slaves and insurmountable debt. Virginia's father, John Hankins, mortgaged the property before his death in 1870. His daughter sold the 1,200-acre estate in 1872 to the mortgage holder to pay off the debt and provide for her brothers' and sisters' education. The family moved to Richmond, where she never married and became a schoolteacher, learned in Latin, French, and German. She also wrote poetry, and an unpublished novel. She died on December 24, 1888, buried in Hollywood Cemetery.

William Allen Warren purchased the estate in 1880 and sold it to his son Charles Allen Warren in 1909. When Charles passed away in 1931, his son, Walker Pegram Warren, inherited the estate. Walker Warren and his wife used Bacon's Castle as a second home until their deaths due to an automobile accident in 1973. The Warrens had no children and no other family to inherit. The mansion, outbuildings, and forty acres of the land were acquired from their estate by the Association for the Preservation of Virginia Antiquities. Virginia State Senator Garland Gray bought the remaining 1,130 acres of the plantation and devoted that to agriculture. Restored, Bacon's Castle became an official Preservation Virginia historic house museum and historic site open for guest visitation.

Bacon's Castle is the oldest building in America, with the oldest formal English garden, too, and is a rare example of American Jacobean architecture. It is the only surviving "high-style" house in the nation from the 17th century. It is one of only three surviving Jacobean great homes in the Western Hemisphere—the other two are in Barbados. It has the oldest formal English garden in North America and is listed on the National Register of Historic Places and was designated as a National Historic Landmark in 1960.

There is one love story with Bacon's Castle that can't be proven and so might be a myth. A young woman in the 1800s met her lover, a farmer, in secret on the side of a cornfield. Her father didn't approve of him. But when she had returned to Bacon's Castle one evening, carrying a candle upstairs to her room, she tripped, and her long hair caught fire from the candle flame. Not wanting her father to know she had been out, she kept quiet and ran from the house, back to the cornfield and her lover. She died in his arms, severely burned.

Bacon's Castle is rife with hauntings, and there are those who say it is the work of the Devil. Someone in connection with another historical building and cemetery, whose wife works at the house, told me a story about some paranormal investigators who had recorded an EVP of a diabolical laugh and voice in the basement (where the large fireplace is). He believes it to be the

Devil himself. Others hold the belief that it is the return of Nathaniel Bacon's men. Although it's unlikely that *every* historic building in Virginia is haunted, there are several that have an undeniably eerie allure to them—like Bacon's Castle. And let's be honest, with so many years of people living there, it could even be members of families who owned the house, slaves, and much more.

Paranormal investigators who have investigated there believe that many of the disembodied spirits are those of the slaves who were subjected to unbearable living conditions. While the mansion was decorated lavishly, the slave quarters hardly had any furniture at all. In place of beds, servants were expected to sleep on piles of hay and rags.

Whatever the spirits may be from, there are numerous sightings, from moaning in the attic to strange noises, floating heads, and unseen entities passing by. The one about the fireball is interesting.

Seen as a pulsating, red ball of fire, it rises from the graveyard of Olde Lawne's Creek Church, which is south of Bacon's Castle. It soars to the castle grounds, "floating or hovering" there before heading back to the Olde Lawne's Creek Church graveyard to vanish.

There were reports of sightings of this fireball over the years. What can it be? Skeptics say it can be explained, while others call it a manifestation of the Devil. One legend tells of a servant a century or two ago, late doing his chores. As he walked home in the dark, a red object appeared out of nowhere and burst, covering him in flames and burning him to death.

Another story talks about hidden money in the castle and that two men had found it years ago while removing some bricks in the fireplace hearth in the second floor's west room. No one had ever found the money, and no one has seen the light since.

A third tale connects it with the spirit of Virginia Hankins, who had lived in the castle and went to the church to meet her sweetheart, Sidney Lanier, many times.

My husband and I took the tour of the place in 2008. Our guide was very knowledgeable, and we learned more than what the history books had ever reported. As for the supernatural, at that time, nothing showed up in my photos and no EVPs on my recorder.

There are those who believe that the fireball is a reminder of the comet that blazed across the night sky centuries ago. Whether it is truth or myth, the fireball and other stories haunting the halls of Bacon's Castle have been lost in the flames of time.

I found a supernatural sighting by the property owner's wife from long ago (no name was ever mentioned—this was in one of L. B. Taylor's ghost books, taken as was written down in research he had found.). She encountered "a sweet white face with large black eyes and parted hair with a white scarf around her head." In yet another inexplicable incident, she discovered her room in disarray. A round burner lamp that usually sat on the table was leaning against a pedestal; a globe was smashed to pieces, a large dictionary lay open on the sofa, and a heavy bookstand had been moved across the room, as if by an unknown force.

There have also been paranormal events happening in modern times. One of the place's interpreters, Frances Richardson, has tried to understand them. When she first started, the house's stairwell had many bloodstained steps, which attested to Bacon Castle's gory past.

Some have seen a disembodied head of an African American woman in the house. During colonial times, the property lodged as many as 300 slaves. There had been eighteen slave quarters initially, but only one still stands today.

Black ink circle around ghost woman's face in the window; I had to add lightened effect so her face would show well.

Black ink circle around ghost dog's face in the window

AUTHOR'S EXPERIENCES DURING GHOST TOUR OF BACON'S CASTLE OCTOBER 2017

I paid to take the ghost tour of the building on October 2, 2016, led by members of the Center for Paranormal Research and Investigations (CPRI).

I walked over to the left side of the house, which was the original section, and started my ghost box up. I began asking questions to see if I would get any answers.

"Is Nathaniel Bacon here at the Allen House?"

A man's voice spoke from my box. "No. He was never here."

Well, that is accurate.

"Are you one of Bacon's men who took over the house?

Are you the only one still here in spirit?" "Yes. There are others."

After that, my battery died, so I took the box and recorder back to the car where Bill waited. I handed both to him and got one of my mini camcorders, but I found the new battery I placed in it had already died. Well, CPRI claims this place is the most haunted in Virginia they ever encountered.

On my way out of the restroom on the newer section of the house I realized I'd not shut the door all the way, so I turned halfway around, when the door closed itself, smacking me lightly on the rear end. I double-checked through a downstairs window to the right of the door, where the investigators were, but I saw no one had left that room, as neither did anyone from the workers' office. Had one of the spirits been upset

I hadn't shut the door as was proper, so they did it themselves? I can't verify that for sure, but it did happen, and I was quick enough to look through that window, which gave me a great vantage point to see if a living person had done it. People began lining up, so I hustled over to join them. Our guide was one of the investigators from CPRI, and he led us around back of the Allen manor to a place that may have been where the slaves lived. He talked about the history of it as well as their findings after they'd investigated the place before he took us inside the main house.

He led us into the older section of the place. It was highly unusual for a home like that, as no others of that kind of building were around at that time. The first room we entered might have been used for entertainment. The guide said he couldn't be sure if the past residents played cards in there, but they had used it for socializing. There had been disembodied voices and unexplained sounds heard in there, even by the paranormal group live or on recordings. People claimed that a chair moved in there, for they would always find it in a different spot where they had left it whenever they returned to the room. The group always marked the chair to see if it moved, but it hadn't the past few years. They had something attached beneath it to catch any sounds if it did move. I asked if they ever had someone sit in the chair and wait to see if it moved, but he admitted that they never thought to do that.

He pointed out that the windows had etchings and markings on the glass, like drawings and writing from past occupants of the Allen house spanning a hundred years. Also, the furnishings in the room were not original to that era, although there were some rooms upstairs that had actual furniture used in that period.

The guide then led us down a flight of stairs to the basement where the kitchen was. Once down there, I asked if any spirits were with us and if they could say something into the small digital camcorder I held. I used it instead of a recorder, to capture EVPs as much as video. Later, I uploaded it and listened but got nothing.

This kitchen is unusual for a southern house in that period, for they usually kept the kitchen in a building outside the main house. Slaves cooked out there and brought in the food to the dining room at mealtimes. But in Bacon's Castle, there is a massive fireplace where they did the cooking. Our guide pointed out that where there is a wall now, there'd once been a door on the left. It must have kept the upstairs warm in the wintertime. They also had their own wine. Now, it is made again and sold in reproduction bottles of the Allen wine.

Our guide pointed out the cross beams in the ceiling and that the wood all around us was the original material from that time. Very remarkable as many historic homes in Virginia had replaced many of their wooden floors and walls by the 21st century. He also pointed out a creepy black shadow on a wall, but it was nothing paranormal but was caused by soot or something similar. It did look like a figure.

He mentioned that people had heard voices and noises where we stood. We were told to remain silent for a few minutes to see if we heard anything. Suddenly, I could hear voices from a room above us, followed by a scraping sound. Our guide said, "Did anyone else hear that besides me? That sounds like it came from the room where the chair is—the scraping would be the chair moving."

Most raised their hands or said they did hear the sound, just as I did.

Because I know I heard voices before the chair movement, I asked, "Is there another tour group up there, maybe? Can you check?"

He called over on his radio, "Anyone in the older section beside us?"

He couldn't get anyone, as for some reason, his walkie- talkie wouldn't work. Was it due to the paranormal or just ordinary reasons?

Later, when I listened to the recording, I heard faint voices and scraping afterward. So, I had caught something, proving I had heard the voices, and not just the chair! Also, after the tour had finished, I asked him to let me know by email if there had been a group of living people in that room, as I said I was sure I heard voices beforehand. When I got an email from him, he stated we were the only group in that section at the time! Had I caught the ghosts socializing, maybe even one moving the chair to sit down in it?

We left that area and followed him upstairs to the garret, as usually we would have already done that, and he didn't want to cheat us of the whole tour. There had been lights and other things seen here. One of the rooms up there always seemed to have a green light hovering inside it. Maybe it was the fireball from the past stories.

A funny story: they heard a noise from the attic space up there, so he had another investigator, Brad, check by going up to it and when Brad opened the door, squirrels scattered out of there. (The man at St. Luke's Church mentioned that there are those museum workers at Bacon's who don't like going into the attic, feeling some awful presence is up in the room).

Our guide pointed out that there had been writings and drawings on the wall made by children in the past. Not unlike kids today might take a marker and draw on the wall of their bedroom.

Done with that area and none of us having any experiences there, we followed him over to the Civil War side of the house. There was a door there with a WIFI camera facing it. They had caught things moving around inside the room it led into, and there had been no one in there. Also, the doorknob would move as if someone was turning it. He admitted to not being able to smell candles burning, and yet, he swore he breathed in the odor of burning candles in the room. To back him up, another investigator, Alan, who is a cop for the state, said he could smell the scent of candle wax melting. No candles are allowed to be burned in the building as it could burn down, and they don't have a sprinkler system because much of the place is original and water can ruin it.

The next time you want to experience history coming alive, try Bacon's Castle. It won't just come alive; you'll be *haunted* by it!

Bacon's Castle at night before the ghost tour

OLD BRICK CHURCH

"Now I know what a ghost is. Unfinished business, that's what."
~Salman Rushdie

Old Brick Church in Surry (Lower Church, Southwark Parish) has been known as the Lawnes Creek Parish Church, and the Lower Surry Church, too. The lower chapel of the Southwark Parish was a brick rectangular room church built in 1754, about a mile northwest of Bacon's Castle.

The Old Brick Church ruins and cemetery

They built the church using brick walls irregularly laid in Flemish bond and English bond with a few glazed headers. The church remained abandoned from the disestablishment of the Church of England in America until 1847. In 1868, a fire destroyed the building, said to have been set by recently freed African slaves following the American Civil War. The thick brick walls kept it standing, though. Its ruins were added to the National Register of Historic Places in 1986.

Typical of the Virginia vernacular churches of the colonial period, prior to its destruction, it no doubt resembled historical Merchant's Hope Church in Prince George County. Its walls kept mainly well preserved until 2003. A large oak tree in the churchyard uprooted by high winds during Hurricane Isabel, fell upon the ruins of the church, collapsing large portions of its walls. The ruins have since been stabilized, and many of the original bricks saved. There are plans to reconstruct the walls and restore the church to its colonial appearance.

Local folklore that goes back more than a century claims that the ruins of the Old Brick Church are haunted. Many credible people, both young and old over several generations, claim to have seen the flying fireball. The story goes that it rises from the church cemetery, forty feet into the air, and heads across the broad fields towards Bacon's Castle. At the time this happened, a church meeting was being held outside in the graveyard. Everyone in attendance claimed to have seen the ball of fire.

AUTHOR'S INVESTIGATION OF THE CEMETERY

Bill drove our car off Route 10 and parked it in a spot by the road. I took my ghost box, recorder, and cameras, and began taking pictures, first of the shell of the church and then the various graves around it.

Done with that, I turned on the box and recorder and went into my investigation.

I asked if anyone had attended the church when it was there, and they were alive. I got several voices saying yes.

I asked, "Have any of you been there when the fireball came out of the graveyard and flew toward Bacon's Castle?"

I had someone say, "Yes, I saw it."

I asked a few more questions, including how they felt about the church ruins. One male voice said he was upset, while a couple of others said it was sad. Except for a few names, I didn't get much, so I thanked them for any answers, shut off the equipment and headed back to the car. Bill and I went for dinner at Anna's as I had the ghost tour that night at Bacon's Castle.

Next time you drive down Route 10 and past the Old Brick Church and graveyard, don't stop. Just leave the dead to their final rest. Unless you happen to see a fireball rise from the graves, then jam your foot hard on the gas pedal and go.

Inside the Old Brick Church ruins

CHIPPOKES PLANTATION STATE PARK

"I saw a ghost once, about 20 years ago. It took the form of someone coming out of a sleeping body and sitting at the foot of the bed."
~Peter Ackroyd

The River House: The oldest house at Chippokes and probably the earliest standing structure in the park.

In 1619, Captain William Powell (Lieutenant Governor of the Jamestown Fort) received a land grant of 550 acres of river frontage on Chippokes Creeks. The name came from Choupocke, a local Algonquin Indian chief. This native chief had been helpful to the early colonists, assisted them in surviving.

Powell bequeathed one of them, his son, the property in 1645. In turn, the son sold it to Henry Bishop a year later.

The new owner purchased adjacent land, making it a total of 1,947 acres.

From 1684 to 1827, Philip Ludwell's family and their descendants owned it. They never resided there, but in nearby Williamsburg across the river, as it was a more beneficial place for a prominent member of London society and of the Governor's Council. When her father died, Lucy Ludwell (who today is said to haunt the house in

Colonial Williamsburg), inherited all his holdings, including the Chippokes Plantation. Two years after her father's death, she married John Paradise, a son of Peter Paradise, who was the former British consul at Salonica in Macedonia. Sadly, Lucy became careless with the fiches she inherited and gained through marriage and became a pauper after John's death in 1795. She left London and returned to the Ludwell-Paradise home in Williamsburg.

The woman became known as Loony Lucy. She would ride in her carriage or walk down the street with servants in tow, acting like royalty and waving like a queen at passersby. It worsened over time as she began going into her neighbors' home and stealing clothing that she wore in "royal" jaunts. Finally, unable to take her shenanigans anymore in 1816, the townspeople hauled her to the nearest asylum, which was the Public Hospital (it opened in 1773 but closed in the 1960s). Before the hospital opened, the insane were cared for at home or confined with vagrants in parish workhouses. Some even became incarcerated in the Public Gaol.

Two years after her incarceration, Lucy died in the asylum. The woman had vowed to return home, but she never did. Then John D. Rockefeller Jr. purchased the building in Williamsburg for the future Colonial Williamsburg attraction, only paying $8,000. When they began restoring the house, workers complained of odd things. One of the workers left a letter that told of tools going missing and papers scattered all over. Documents needed to renovate the place couldn't be found. Pounding noises came from empty rooms, and water would be turned on and off, even splashing in the water as if someone was playing in it. Eventually, they finished the work, and it opened as an exhibition in April 1935, four months after the restoration. The building exhibited Abby Aldrich Rockefeller's folk-art collection at one time.

Chippokes has been a working farm for more than 350 years. In the 17th and 18th centuries, the produce grown on the plantation were corn, apples, grain, and tobacco, and becoming tobacco and peanut in the 19th and 20th centuries, plus a variety of crops as well as livestock.

Albert C. Jones became the owner in 1837. His family plot is several miles south of the park, along Route 10. It is surrounded by crumbling brick walls. As the first owner to reside on the plantation, he lived in the River House until 1854, when he built a larger mansion in the Classical Italianate style. It is known as the Jones-Stewart Mansion. The place had several early outbuildings and farm structures. Jones preferred living in the River House; it gave him a bird's-eye view over several slave quarters. Today, one of those slave homes became a place for the park manager to stay. The property remained in the Jones family until 1916. Other places became homes for the former slaves turned sharecroppers. The buildings and the mansion itself had fallen into disrepair and went to public auction. Mr. and Mrs. Victor Stewart purchased it and restored it over four decades to its former glory. When Victor Stewart passed away, his wife donated it to the Commonwealth of Virginia for a state park in

1967. As one of the requirements, she stated to keep the mansion's furnishings as they were when she and her husband lived there.

The park has woods, fertile fields, and a sandy beach at the river's edge. There are fossil hikes, guided canoe tours, fishing programs, and ranger-led activities, along with a swimming pool, children's playground, and more than 12 miles of trails for hiking, biking, and horseback riding. Besides the cabins to stay in, there is a full-service campground with electric and water hookups, a dump station, and a bathhouse. Plus, the mansion and the other rental facilities are available for weddings and special events. The park is on the National Register of Historic Places and is an active farm.

THE GHOST STORIES

One of the haunts believed to make their presence known is Mrs. Stewart herself. One of the activities attributed to her happened to a local young lady. After the mansion closed for the day, she had sat down on the front steps. Suddenly, from behind, she heard footsteps coming down, and when she turned to see which park employee was making the sounds, she saw nothing, though the footsteps drew closer and closer. She bolted for her car, got in, and drove away.

A volunteer tour guide in 1997 was alone inside the mansion on a rainy day. She began working on some sewing when suddenly, the front door flew open. The room grew bone-chilling cold, and she saw hair and fabric, but not a face or human form, passing by her. It headed toward a closed double glass door and passed through them. Many assumed this had been Mrs. Stewart as the extensive renovation being done on the house might have upset her.

Another story concerned one of the docents at the Jones- Stewart Mansion, Joan, who was there for tours one night, but no one showed up due to the dark and nasty weather. Her husband, Bill, was there with her, and he ran into town to pick up a takeout pizza for them, leaving her alone. She sat in a chair in the front hall when suddenly, the door flew open, letting in the heavy rain and wind. She also swore something like mist and hair went down the hall and out the other side. Joan found herself unable to get up to close the door. She didn't remember seeing a face, but she knew something was there, something human-sized, a display of ethereal loveliness.

Though they work to keep quiet about the paranormal activity, some tales slip out, like those about shadowy apparitions seen in the chairs on the side porch. Park guests always asked about the smiling people dressed in period clothing seen rocking on those chairs. In the beginning, the docents were puzzled and would look out, finding no one, but over time, they became used to these ghosts that are presumed to be the Stewarts.

Many tour guests over the years insist they can smell the aroma of tobacco smoke in the study on the first floor. Docents would go into the room, even pick up Mr. Stewart's pipe on display there, finding it cold and with no hint of an odor.

Another phenomenon concerns the books: If a book is borrowed and left elsewhere, that volume is always mysteriously placed back to the niche it came from, and never by any of the volunteers. Obviously, even after death, one of the Stewarts like their books put back where they belong.

The Friends of Chippokes Plantation (formed in 1988) spend thousands of hours dedicated to making the park a pleasant place for visitors. Of course, they are witnesses to much of the paranormal activity, too. One of these experiences happened to a volunteer named David in the detached two-story brick kitchen where many of the park's hearth cooking demonstrations occur. He heard flute music from upstairs. Impossible, unless someone had left a radio on, so he climbed the stairs to turn it off. Except once he was up there, he couldn't find a radio or anything else that could make that noise. And yet, as he listened, he swore it came from a flute. But no one else was there. It hit him that he was experiencing ghostly activity. Frightened, he bolted downstairs, out the kitchen door, and across the yard until he ran into other volunteers. He asked them if they could hear the music, and the rest knew it could only be one of the park's haunts.

David's mother, Mrs. Van den Brink, a park volunteer also, had many encounters with the spirits there. There had been the time when she and her husband worked the Christmas show at the park. Alone at the time, she sat in the brick kitchen reading a newspaper when the sound of footsteps outside came to her ears. Since that might mean a park guest, she peeked out, but didn't see a soul.

Another location is the Old Smith House. It, too, has its ghostly stories. Over a hundred and fifty years ago, it served as the slave quarters. Former Park Manager Danette Poole and her children had many encounters here. Like the time Poole had just given birth to her one son. She fell ill, and so her sister-in-law came to be a caregiver until she got well. Because the woman's year-and-a-half-old son was missing her, her husband brought him to her. When he got there, he acted agitated. Both she and Mrs. Poole couldn't understand why, as he always had a cheerful disposition. Feeling much better and able to attend to her own baby, Mrs. Poole told her sister-in-law to go upstairs with her son and lie down with him, hoping she could get him to fall asleep. After sleeping for a while, the sister-in-law awoke. She stared over at her son, finding him smiling while staring up at the ceiling and talking to himself. But as she rolled over, she saw an African American gentleman dressed all in white. He put his finger to his lips as if to shush her, then began talking to her son. Although she didn't hear anything, whatever he did appeared to comfort her boy, for he no longer acted anxious. Suddenly, the man dissipated before their eyes. She snatched up her son and hastened downstairs to tell Mrs. Poole what had happened to her. Until she and her son left, the boy remained at peace.

One night after she tucked her son into his bed, Mrs.

Poole caught him staring at the room's window. "Are you all right, Jerry?"

He replied, "I'm fine, Mama. Just watching the lady brushing the hair of the other lady in the chair."

She left him alone and went back to sleep in her bed. But the next morning at breakfast, she asked Jerry to tell her about the women. He described clothing that sounded Colonial and that they were brushing each other's long tresses.

It appears not even the rental cabins are free of spookiness. Three of the buildings were once homes of the Osbornes, the Browns, and the Spratleys who were brought to the area as slaves originating from Angola in Africa before being freed to become tenant farmers, and then, staff members at the park. In the 1990s, the park established journals for those staying there to share their experiences.

One of these, Philip Jones from New York, had written he came there after finding out that his ancestors came from Angola four hundred years ago. They were the first African slaves held on a Spanish frigate that a ship from the Virginia Company of London and a Dutch vessel together had captured. Thinking that they had gold, silver, or even food, instead, they found a hold jammed with his ancestors and other Africans. Adverse winds took them to Jamestown, with only 22 slaves left. Most had been tossed overboard due to a lack of food. Philip had learned his ancestors eventually ended up working for Chippokes Park. That was why he was there. He mentioned further in the journal that his son and granddaughter stayed in the Spratley House, which had belonged to his cousin. He, his daughter, two granddaughters, and one grandson stayed in another cousin's place, the Brown House. He accounted that spirits haunted the buildings, and that his grandmother Louise Osborne had told him stories about strange things and sounds she couldn't explain. One night after a trip to Virginia Beach, they found people at a table, eating. Philip said they wondered who the visitors were and why they were in their cabin when the strangers vanished. Another time, after misbehaving, one of his granddaughters had been sent upstairs. After a lamp fell off a table, she tried to scream but couldn't. Instead, a spectral image formed out of the wall and scolded her. The girl scrambled downstairs to tell her story and remained there, behaving all night, so she didn't have to go back upstairs.

Other guests who stayed at the Spratley House in October 2006 to enjoy fall in the park went for a hike, but foul weather interrupted it, and they came back to the cabin, remaining there for most of their stay. They wrote in the journal that the bed shook all night, the doors would swing open and close by themselves, and they would hear odd noises. The front door locked itself one time, the electricity flickered and the thermostat changed by itself.

Their last entry, close to Halloween, stated, "Beware! This cabin's haunted! The bed shakes; it did it for me. Pennies appear to drop from the ceiling. The rocking chair rocks by itself, and no one is in it, plus the electricity flickers! Even the door locks on its own! So, beware!" Now, this could be taken with a grain of salt, or maybe it did happen to the couple. But this is one story that has me wondering about the truth.

Another family staying there had read the ghost stories and decided they would test the ghost, or ghosts. Before they left for the park, they left a circle of pennies on the kitchen table. When they returned, they found the pennies rearranged in a square shape.

Before the year's end, accounts filled the journal, ranging from strange noises to freaked out pets to taps above and below the beds, to even objects mysteriously rearranged, and sightings of entities.

Another cabin, the Brown House, had first been the residence of the overseer. Nowadays, spirit activity includes rocking chairs moving to other spots in the room when no living person has touched them. There are those guests who arrive at Cabin 2 to find a family enjoying a meal at the kitchen table. Suddenly, these strangers vanished before their eyes. Or when the guests heard noises coming from inside, they knocked on the door then walked inside to find no one. There is even some person seen looking out the second-story window on repeated occasions.

Mrs. Roberg, the housekeeper, was with her daughter, Abigail, to clean the cabin. Abigail worked upstairs and laid her iPod on the bed, only walking a few feet away. Its screen went blank and into lock mode. As she attended to her duties, the iPod lit up. She watched as her private passcode was punched in. Screaming in terror, she fled downstairs. It appears that even ghosts like to go online, maybe to check out Facebook or watch a movie.

SMITH'S FORT PLANTATION

"History is the memory of time, the life of the dead, and the happiness of the living."
~John Smith

Smith's Fort Plantation House

Smith's Fort was built on Gray's Creek in Surry by 1609, on Hog Island (today it holds a wildlife management area) which Colonists used to raise hogs. The site still has earthworks of Captain John Smith's proposed "New Fort." It is located directly across the James River from Jamestown. The unfinished fort site was only partially completed in 1609 before being abandoned. Captain John Smith built a fort on the south side of the James River as a retreat position if ever Jamestown was attacked by Virginia Indians or the Spanish.

The story and half brick manor house sits on land given by Chief Wahunsenacawh (Powhatan) as a dowry for his daughter Pocahontas' marriage to John Rolfe in 1614. As we know, the couple and their son went to England, where she died and was buried. The couple's son, Thomas Rolfe, inherited the land, and sometime later in the seventeenth century, another owner, Thomas Warren, built a house on the property. The house that now occupies the site was first called the John Rolfe House but is now known as the Rolfe-Warren House, probably dates to the mid-eighteenth century, when it served as the home of the Jacob Faulcon family.

It is a beautifully restored 18th-century manor style building, built on the property by Jacob Faulcon between 1751 and 1756. The home is made of Flemish Bond brick and has a charming interior that retains much of its original woodwork, like the "Blue Room," which has the original arched cupboards with butterfly shelving. The gabled roof has dormer windows. The home features examples of early American and English period furnishings from the late 16th through the early 18th centuries. Much of the interior still has the original woodwork. There are historic Virginia flower gardens by the Garden Club of Virginia display plants found in the colonial gardens of Williamsburg and Yorktown. Preservation Virginia acquired Smith's Fort in 1933 after John D. Rockefeller Jr. restored it. Smith's Fort became listed on the Virginia Landmarks Register on October 16, 1973, and with the National Register of Historic Places on November 14, 1973.

AUTHOR'S VISIT AND INVESTIGATION

Bill drove us to Smith's Fort Plantation by GPS. We almost missed the driveway, but we found it and drove up it to park near the house. I did take the tour inside the house. The place was charming, and the guide knowledgeable. I even bought a couple of postcards.

I did a ghost box session and after that, an EVP one, to see what I could get, if anything, about any spirits lingering from Smith's Fort, the house and maybe even any natives. The tour guide had told me she doubted the place was haunted, unlike Preservation Virginia's other building in Surry, Bacon's Castle.

I did the ghost box first and turned it on. "Any spirits still lingering here?"

A male voice uttered from the box, "Yes."

"Can you give me a name?" I said again, "A name." No answer.

I asked again. A woman's voice said something, but it was low and static also muffled it.

I tried another question. "Did you come from Jamestown?"

A male voice said, "Yes." Another voice said, "Virginia."

I asked how far from where I stood were the remains of Smith's second fort. A different male voice said, "Three."

Three what? Yards? Feet? Miles? Not helpful.

"Are there spirits still haunting the house on this land?" A male voice said, "Ghosts."

Another voice uttered, "Virginia."

I was excited as I heard the ghost and Virginia clearly and exclaimed, "Ghosts! Did you say ghosts?"

The male voice again replied, "Ghosts." A female voice said, "Haunted Virginia."

Okay, that felt creepy to me. Virginia being said twice, the word, ghosts, too, and even more so, the woman using the phrase, Haunted Virginia.

I said thanks and shut off the box, doing a quick EVP session, but got nothing, except a cow mooing (as there were cows in the pasture next door) and a thump. The thump sounded close to me, and I cannot say for sure if that was paranormal.

I shut everything off and headed back to the car to hand all equipment to Bill before I went up to the house to take the tour. Afterward, I stopped by the field of flowers planted for butterflies that the tour guide told me about, took some pictures, and paid some money into a box for picking a couple of the flowers to take home. So many insects are disappearing with climate change, and it was great that someone was doing this.

Thinking this leads to where John Smith had tried to build the second fort after Jamestown

A SURRY GHOST STORY

"In Eastern culture, people see ghosts, people talk about ghosts... it's just accepted. And in Western culture it's just not."
~Jessica Alba

As author Deborah Painter reported in her foreword of this book, she had read the account of an old, uninhabited home at Cabin Point, Surry, which was owned by the sister of a young merchant seaman from Norfolk. The sister had intended to restore it as a summer vacation home. The seaman and a friend hitchhiked so that one of them could have a date with a Cabin Point girl. Afterward, both men planned to get a good night's sleep at the old place but received little sleep because they thought they heard horses and men on the dark grounds, yet neither one never saw anything. One of them reported having a bizarre dream encounter with a regretful old lady. They found that the lady was connected to Baron von Steuben, a Major General in the Continental Army during the Revolutionary War.

ISLE OF WIGHT

"Some places speak distinctly. Certain dark gardens cry aloud for a murder; certain old houses demand to be haunted; certain coasts are set apart for shipwreck."
~Robert Louis Stevenson

Isle of Wight County is a county located in the Hampton Roads region of the state of Virginia. It was named after the Isle of Wight, along the Solent in England, from where many of its early colonists came.

The Warraskoyak were a tribe of the Powhatan Confederacy, who had three towns in the area of modern Smithfield. English colonists drove the Warraskoyak from their villages in 1622 and 1627, as part of their reprisals for the Great Massacre of 1622, in which the Native Americans had decimated English settlements, hoping to drive them out of their territory.

Isle of Wight County features two incorporated towns, Smithfield and Windsor. The first courthouse for the county was built in Smithfield in 1750. The original courthouse and its tavern, Smithfield Inn, still stand. People can still stay overnight in the inn.

As the county population developed, leaders decided they needed a county seat near the center of the area, so they built a new courthouse in 1800. The 1800 brick courthouse and its associated tavern (Boykin's Tavern) are still standing today, as are the 1822 clerk's offices nearby. The 1800 courthouse is used daily, serving as the government chambers for the Board of Supervisors, as well as the meeting hall for the School Board. The chambers are sometimes used as a court for civil trials if the new courthouse is entirely in use. The new courthouse opened in 2010; it is across the street from the sheriff's office and county offices complex.

SMITHFIELD

Towns are excrescences, gray fluxions, where men, hurrying to find one another, have lost themselves.
~E. M. Forster

The town of Smithfield's bustling wharf harbor became a popular destination for clipper ships bringing goods from the old world to the new, and all due to the hams and peanuts that have made Smithfield world famous. And at one time, Edward Teach, aka the pirate, Blackbeard, and his flotilla of ships, was said to have hidden in an inlet near what would become the area.

Looking down Main Street in Historic Smithfield

There's the Smithfield Inn, Mansion on the Main Bed and Breakfast, and Smithfield Station for places to stay overnight. Attractions in Smithfield include Old Courthouse of 1750, modeled after the Capitol Building in Colonial Williamsburg. The Smithfield & Isle of Wight Visitor's Center can steer a person right, and they will give you an Old Town Walking Tour map that covers over fifty buildings of historical significance. You can visit places and get a good exercise in. And if you get hungry, there is Taste of Smithfield, The Cockeyed Rooster, Sista's Cafe, Smithfield Gourmet Bakery and Café, William Rand Tavern, Smithfield Ice Cream Parlor, and many other eateries.

You can also drive to Fort Boykin Historic Park, St. Luke's Church, Fort Huger, or arrange a visit to Mill Swamp Indian Horse Farm, where you can see where the nearly extinct Corolla Spanish Mustangs from the Outer Banks are bred and trained.

The town of Smithfield is only 10.1 miles. Both town and county were first colonized in 1634. Located on the banks of the Pagan River and lying on the opposite shore of the James River, across from Jamestown, the area became discovered by Captain John Smith and other early settlers. Smithfield and surrounding counties saw action during the Revolutionary War and Civil War, mainly because of its proximity to the James River. The Virginia Landmarks Register mentions that Smithfield may be the most preserved of Virginia's ports. Virginia Reviews had remarked it is one of the prettiest towns in the Commonwealth and also named as one of fifty best small southern towns.

The town began in trade and commerce but ultimately ended up with four plants devoted to the art of curing the world-famous Smithfield Ham, headquartered in Smithfield. The company runs facilities in 26 U.S. states, including the largest slaughterhouse and meat-processing plant in the world, located in Tar Heel, North Carolina. Smithfield was founded in 1936 by Joseph W. Luter Sr. and his son, Joseph W. Luter Jr., as the Smithfield Packing Company. From 1981, the company purchased companies such as Eckrich, Farmland Foods of Kansas, Gwaltney of Smithfield, John Morrell and Co, Murphy Family Farms of North Carolina, and Premium Standard Farms. It was able to grow as a result of its highly industrialized pig production, raising the animals using a vertical integration system of production that enables the company to control their development from conception to packing. Smithfield sells its products under a variety of brand names, including Cook's Ham, Gwaltney, John Morrell, Krakus Ham, Patrick Cudahy, Smithfield, and Stefano's. The company also operates The Genuine Smithfield Ham Shoppe and a restaurant, Taste of Smithfield, both in Smithfield. On March 21, 2003, they had the biggest ham biscuit accepted for the Guinness World Records. Smithfield was purchased in 2013 by Chinese-based and state-owned holding company Shuanghui International Holdings Ltd. Shuanghui Group is the world's largest pork producer and processor.

There is the Isle of Wright County Museum in Smithfield. It has the oldest, edible, cured ham. This ham was cured in 1902 by a local pork processor, Pembroke D. Gwaltney Jr, but it was misplaced and forgotten only to be rediscovered many years later. Pembroke outfitted the ham with a brass collar, called it his "pet ham," and showed it to customers as proof of his ability to preserve meat without refrigeration. His company became famous because of the ham and not long afterward, to fuse with the pork behemoth Smithfield Foods.

It outlasted its tireless promoter, who passed away in 1936, and was donated to the museum by one of Pembroke's grandchildren in 1985. One of the Isle of Wight County Museum curator's jobs is to keep the ham edible by keeping it free of bugs and mold. The ham shares a particularly climate-controlled case with two other famous hams, one of them said to be the world's largest. It was featured in *Ripley's Believe It or Not* in 1929, 1932 and 2003. The year 2002 marked the ham's 100th anniversary. No matter its age, the ham is not the oldest thing in the museum. That honor goes to the world's oldest peanut, picked by Gwaltney's father, P.D. Gwaltney, Sr. Gwaltney Sr. happened to be called the "Peanut King," too. Although unlike the ham, I would advise against testing the peanut's edibility, as the museum makes no claim that it still is good.

Besides the museum, Smithfield has Windsor Castle Park, Historic Luke's Church, the Arts Center@319, and the Old Courthouse of 1750. The Old Courthouse of 1750 was modeled after the Capitol Building in Colonial Williamsburg originally. They restored the building to its original beautiful state. Also connected to Smithfield and Isle of Wight area are Historic Fort Huger, Fort Boykin Historic Park, Boykin's Tavern, and the Schoolhouse Museum. There's also Darden's Country Store and Smokehouse. Smithfield Station, Waterfront Inn and Restaurant, Marina and Conference Center, the Smithfield Inn, plus the Mansion on Main Bed and Breakfast (historic Victorian built in 1889).

Some may have ghostly tales; some are nothing more than cool places to visit.

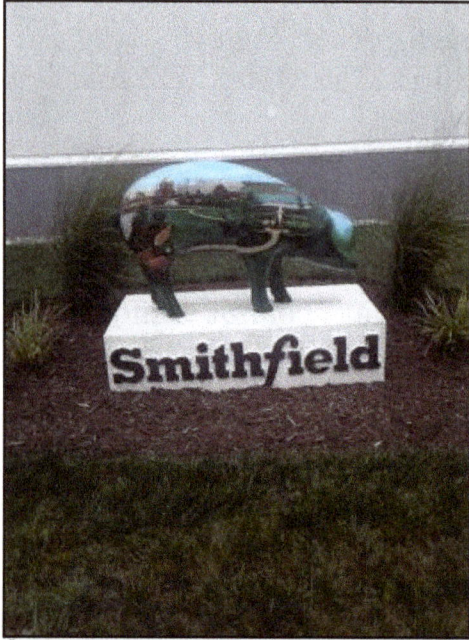

A Smithfield pig statue (one of several in town) outside
of the Smithfield Packing Company

Isle of Wight Museum in Smithfield

The oldest ham which has been in the Guinness Book of
Records is in the Isle of Wight Museum.

A SMITHFIELD GHOST STORY

"Apparitions are often confused with hauntings.
The difference is that apparitions are 'live'
(intelligent consciousness) and hauntings are
'recordings.'"
~Loyd Auerbach

Too short to put it in its own chapter, so I am connecting it to the Smithfield chapter, at the end.

This came from another post online in 2016, where the person says they live on Cedar Street in Smithfield, and that their house may be haunted. The family always hears footsteps upstairs. Another encounter happened the year before. The girl's mother put her phone down on the couch, and five seconds later, it flew off the couch. It scared them both, as they were the only people in the house at that time—at least, living ones.

SMITHFIELD STATION

"The first ghost story I ever heard was from my
mother."
~Jenna Wortham

In 1983, Ron and Tina Pack took a boat cruise with friends in the upper Chesapeake Bay, and they decided that their newly adopted town of Smithfield was every bit as lovely as the favored destination points of the upper bay communities. This became a dream to establish Smithfield as a historic destination just as nice as the neighboring waterfront communities.

Smithfield Station

Smithfield Station's Traditional Rooms are located in The Inn, which is built entirely over the water and sits on 110 piles that are 88 feet long. Modeled after the old Coast Guard lifesaving stations along the coast of Virginia and Outer Banks of North Carolina, in November of 1986, the Pack family completed construction on the main building.

They opened the restaurant, hotel, and marina. This includes a hundred-and-fifty-seat dining room, fifteen hotel rooms, and a marina.

The award-winning restaurant at Smithfield Station was designed to provide a dining experience that takes advantage of Smithfield's two best-known culinary commodities: Smithfield ham, and fresh local seafood. The truly unique dining experience is accented by the scenic river views, full-service bar, outdoor waterside seating, and a wide variety of local entertainment and live music.

Change is the only constant with the Pack family, and in 1994, Smithfield Station constructed and opened the now famous Lighthouse at Smithfield Station. The Lighthouse is the only one on the East Coast that offers overnight accommodation and is a must-stay for any lighthouse enthusiast. The Lighthouse is a reproduction of the one from Hoopers Strait in Maryland that is now a part of the Maritime Museum in St. Michael's, Maryland. Several historic lighthouses of similar design were constructed on the James River, but all have been destroyed.

In 2001, the Pack's transformed one of the dining rooms and tiny bars into The Inner Banks (IBX), a more informal bar and grille with its own menu and live entertainment. IBX has become a favorite watering hole for locals and visitors alike.

In 2001 and 2003 respectively, a new generation of Packs, Randy and Brian, became fully involved with the business. With the addition of these two brothers, it seemed the ideal time to expand Smithfield Station with the creation of the Lodge. The Lodge added 22 deluxe luxury rooms to the inn. These rooms were designed to be a world- class lodging experience featuring hand-crafted cherry wood furniture, upgraded bedding and linens, oversized bathrooms (some featuring Jacuzzi tubs), electric fireplaces, HD LCD Flat Panel TVs, granite accents, and most with private walkout balconies. In addition to the rooms, the lodge building also added the much-needed hotel lobby, boardwalk retail shops, conference rooms, elevator, and additional marina slips.

Smithfield Station is still growing today as the Packs continue to look for new ways to deliver the ultimate travel experience for their guests. They continuously evaluate the amenities, services, and facilities, and upgrade to guarantee the best that historic Smithfield has to offer.

The Chesapeake Bay Magazine recognized The Smithfield Station's restaurant with four separate Best of the Bay awards: Best Restaurant for Crab Cakes, Best Restaurant for a Gourmet Meal, Best Restaurant for the Whole Family, and Best Dockside Bar.

Smithfield Station appears not only to be popular with the living but the dead, too. According to locals, the apparition of a man has been often seen sitting at the bar late at night, long past closing time. Some have even suggested that he's the spirit of a person who drowned long ago in the river behind the building after leaving the bar.

SMITHFIELD INN

"Ghosts" are people, or part of people, anyway, and thus governed by emotional stimuli; they do not perform like trained circus animals, just to please a group of skeptics or sensation seekers. Then too, one should remember that an apparition is really a re-enactment of an earlier emotional experience, and rather a personal matter. A sympathetic visitor would encourage it; a hostile onlooker inhibits it."
~Hans Holzer

Smithfield Inn

Smithfield Inn is older than the Alamo in Texas and Philadelphia's Independence Hall. Built in 1752, unlike many "George Washington slept here" stories, he did sleep there. Smithfield's bustling wharf harbor became a popular destination for clipper ships bringing goods from the old world to the new, and all due to the hams and peanuts that have made Smithfield world famous.

Because of that, there was a need to serve travelers, along with others who journeyed over the main stagecoach route from Norfolk to Richmond, later this included by steamboat and motorcar. The original residence was converted to an Inn and Tavern in 1759 and after more than

250 years, southern hospitality and charm still defines the "Old Inn on Main Street." Over the years, changes like raising the roof to a full second story in 1870, part of bringing the Inn back from disrepair after the Civil War, and a major renovation by the Sykes family in 1922, along with adding the long kitchen and dining room wing and enlarging the porch across the entire front, having taken place. The Sykes Inn grew famous for its signature home-cooked meals and relaxed atmosphere.

Today, the owner of Smithfield Foods owns the Smithfield Inn. The inn offers five historic, one-of-a-kind bed & breakfast suites on the second floor. Each one has a private bath, sitting room, and bedroom with a queen size bed. That is, except for the Todd Suite, which has a king. The Luter and Todd Suites have working gas fireplaces. The adjacent Garden House offers three charming rooms. Two bedrooms in one, and two with king-size beds. Besides all that comfort, all rooms come with robes, high-speed Internet connection, LCD TVs, and phones with free local calls. The rates include a made-to- order Southern-style breakfast for lodging guests only.

Is it haunted? I did my research online and in books, and I read that in the Smithfield Inn, there is a painting of a woman whose family originally owned the building. An employee told the person who wrote the article that when they leave for the night, the picture is upside right, but when they arrive in the morning, it is upside down. Is this true? I have no evidence to say it is, but it is still an interesting ghost story, or if the painting is real, maybe it just needs a better hanging space.

Another story is that a former innkeeper, Mrs. Sykes, haunts it. Again, I have no proof, but these do make for great ghost stories.

You can stay at the Smithfield Inn. Just check their website to see what they have. But if someone knocks at the door to your room and you open it to see who it is and no one is standing there, it might just be Mrs. Sykes checking to make sure your room is fine with you. You can't keep a good innkeeper down.

SMITHFIELD BAKERY AND CAFÉ

"Pastries are a baker's remedy for all ills."
~Anthony T. Hincks

This bakery has more than pastries, cupcakes, and sandwiches, it has spirits, too!

Bill and I attended the Fort Clifton Festival in Colonial Heights on Mother's Day 2016, and a vendor there told me that an employee at the bakery in Smithfield said they had ghosts of Confederate soldiers walking across their floors all the time. So, as we drove down on Friday, August 12, 2015, for the Suffolk Mystery Authors Festival, we turned left off Route 10 and drove down Main Street, parking across the street from the ice cream parlor. After breakfast at A Taste of Smithfield, I walked down to the Mansion on Main to take some pictures of it and the Smithfield Inn, plus a couple of other potentially haunted spots. Bill then picked me up as it had grown hotter, and he parked curbside by the bakery.

The bakery is located at 218 Main Street. When I walked inside for the first time, I saw people eating at tables and when I turned left, I saw a glass case full of pastries, cookies, and more. I went ahead and bought two Danish pastries. Mine had cheese on each side, while the one I picked for my husband had cheese on one side, the other, cherry. The employees admitted that the building might be haunted and that the employee who talked to the jam and jellies lady might be this man who claims he could see ghosts and says he saw the ones in the bakery. But he was off that day. One young woman admitted to never seeing or hearing anything in the place, but she said she never saw anything anywhere. The man who worked with her admitted that sometimes he heard things that sounded out of the ordinary. But again, since the equipment was on, he thought that could be the explanation.

They gave me a business card to contact the owner, told me to get her at the catering number, as she could help me more.

The building was built in the early 1800's by local businessman Jack Blair, and built upon one of the ten original land grants from England in 1734. The building operated as a brick storehouse for over 20 years. Next, it became a pharmacy from 1834 until the late 1970's. After that, various types of businesses were housed in it. Smithfield Gourmet Bakery and Cafe have operated in the building since 1993, devoting time and money to preserve this historical landmark for the future. The third floor of the building is fully restored, has original pine floors, exposed brick walls, and original windows. It currently serves as a dining room for dinner as well as for special catered events. If you go inside the bakery and café for a quick bite to eat, even a sweet treat, don't be shocked if a Civil War soldier walks by you, vanishing. Death can be a hungry business.

WINDSOR CASTLE PARK

"The boundaries which divide Life from Death are at best shadowy and vague. Who shall say where the one ends, and where the other begins?"
~Edgar Allan Poe

Parts of Windsor Castle and its former plantation are now part of a 208-acre public park overlooking the Pagan River in the town of Smithfield. Once, it was a part of a 1,450-acre parcel patented by Arthur Smith on September 10, 1637, and was formerly known as

Warraskoyack Shire. Today, Windsor Castle Park (only 208 acres) is a park with the circa 1725 manor house and its eleven buildings. Arthur Smith is the ancestor of Smithfield's founder, Arthur Smith IV. It became a Virginia Landmarks Register and part of the National Register of Historic Places of the National Park Service, United States Department of the Interior, in August 2000. The house was modified in the early 1800s.

The manor house at Windsor Castle Park

Archeological evidence proves that the slave quarters once stood where the vineyards now occupy.

The Warraskoyack Indians first occupied this area. Archaeological evidence of activity had been found in front of the house, close to the river.

Arthur Smith was the third son of Arthur Smith of Blackmore, Essex, England. His date of arrival in Virginia is unknown. He represented the district at the House of Burgesses from 1644 to

1645. Father of five children, Thomas, Arthur, Richard, Jane, and George, Smith died in 1645. His request was to be "buried in the garden by my late and beloved wife." Archaeologists have yet to find evidence of the first house on the 159-acre tract where the current house, outbuildings, and cemetery sit.

Arthur Smith II, 1638-1697, inherited the property from his father in 1645. He was the county justice from 1675 to 1680, a colonel in the militia in 1680, and a representative to the House of Burgess in 1685. He married Sarah Jackson, and they had five children: Thomas, George, Arthur, Mary, and Jane.

Arthur Smith III inherited the property in 1697. He was the county justice from 1702 to 1714 and a member of the vestry at the Old Brick Church from 1733 to 1740. He married Mary Bromfield, and they had six children: Arthur, Thomas, Martha, Jane, Olive, and Mary. He died in 1742.

Arthur Smith IV inherited the estate in 1742. In 1750, he petitioned the General Assembly to dock his entailed estate to create a town which he would call Smithfield. The town was established in 1752 with four streets and 72 lots. He married Elizabeth Bray-Allen, but he died without children in 1755.

Based on the material evidence found in cellar excavations and the style of brickwork, archaeologists believe that the current house had begun by 1740—part of the cellar dates to a previous structure, perhaps an earlier house.

Thomas Smith inherited the estate from his uncle in 1755. Thomas was the son of Arthur IV's brother, Thomas. He married Elizabeth Waddrop, and they had six children: Arthur, Elizabeth, Sarah, Fanny, Leila, and Jenny. Thomas died in 1799.

Arthur Smith V inherited the estate from his father in 1799. He was a captain during the War of 1812, a colonel in the militia and a member of the House of Delegates from 1818 to 1820 and from 1837 to 1838. He studied law at the College of William & Mary and never married. Arthur V sold the manor house and plantation to Watson P. Jordan on October 17, 1838.

Other owners of the house included William P. Jordan, his son, Filmore Jordan, who inherited it but sold it on January 1, 1884, to Jeremiah Johnson. The deed for the estate refers to the site as "the Smith tract or Windsor Castle." First mention of this house as Windsor Castle, though there is no explanation anywhere the reason for the name. Jeremiah married Antoinette Vick in 1868 and had two daughters. The youngest daughter, Effie, married Charles Samuel Betts. When her father passed away, they inherited the house upon his death. Their son, Charles Samuel Betts Jr., owned the house until 1977.

The cemetery has two existing markers—dated 1870 and 1921. There is no doubt that this may have been the 18th century Arthur Smith family cemetery. Though upon closer examination of the site, the cemetery may date back to the 17th century as well. When Arthur Smith V sold the property to Watson P. Jordan in 1838, he reserved the right to enter the burial ground.

Joseph W. Luter III donated $5 million to the town for the purchase and development of Windsor Castle and its surrounding 208 acres as a park in 2007. The 46 acres immediately surrounding the manor house are protected by a historic easement controlled by the state of Virginia. The park opened May 22, 2010, during a ceremony officiated by the Virginia Governor Bob McDonnell. The park features hiking trails, a dog park, a mountain bike trail, a fishing pier, and a canoe launch. The manor house and the farm buildings overlook the junction of Cypress Creek and the Pagan River.

THE AUTHOR'S VISIT AND INVESTIGATION OCTOBER 24, 2019

I left Bill, who parked in the parking lot of the park area, and walked up the road to where the manor house and farm buildings stood. I snapped various shots of the house and the farm buildings on the premises. You never know where or how you might capture a ghostly image.

Done with that, I headed down toward the Pagan River and the wooden dock. I settled in and snapped some great shots of the river in both directions. Then, I turned on my digital recorder, and next, the ghost box, to begin a session. I immediately asked, "Are there any spirits of the families who lived in the house still hanging around? Give me some names?"

A male voice said "Brett" three times. "How many spirits are with me right now?"

What sounded like a man replied from the box, "10." "Are you all or most of you connected to the house?" A woman answered, "Yes."

I wish she would say all or how many were connected, but they never make it easy, or maybe it is hard for them.

An idea came to me, so I asked, "Anyone died in the Pagan River by drowning?"

A man blurted out, "Yes." "How long ago was this?" He said, "Eight."

Eight years or months? "What's your name—the man that drowned?"

He replied, but it was low and muffled.

"Was it from the bridge I can see from here—near Smithfield Station? Did you fall from there?"

"Jumped."

That word sent chills up my spine, as I heard this from my laptop, and I am glad I hadn't during that time. Was this the male spirit seen at Smithfield Station, the one they said fell into the river and drowned?

Because I hadn't precisely heard him live at that time, I went on. "Did you fall from the bridge?"

"No."

I had heard that 'no' and went on with other questions. Again, sort of proof that the poor guy may have killed himself at the time of the session.

I asked anyone from the family who once lived in the manor house what they did while alive. A male voice said, "Farming."

I asked if any Confederate soldier ghosts were with me. Later, as I listened at home, I heard 'three' uttered three times.

Finally, I said goodbye, and I got a farewell from a male spirit from the box.

I called Bill on my phone and got him to come get me. We drove away, and I didn't look back to see if anyone insubstantial watched us leave.

Next time you come to Windsor Park to jog or walk the trails, and you get that feeling of someone or something watching you, the dead are still hanging around their land, making sure it is being properly maintained.

IVY HILL CEMETERY

"O Death, rock me asleep, bring me to quiet rest, let pass my weary guiltless ghost out of my careful breast."
~Anne Boleyn

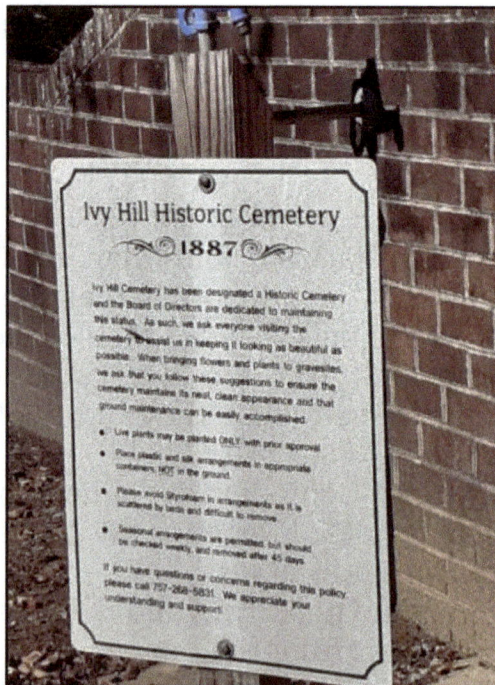

The Ivy Hill Historic Cemetery sign at the brick gates

Ivy Hill Cemetery is a historic rural cemetery and national historic district located at 451 N Church Street, Smithfield, Isle of Wight County, Virginia. Established in 1886, it is a privately-owned cemetery, with grave markers dating from the mid-19th century to the present day. The cemetery is close to the Smithfield Foods Packing plant. It is a Virginia Landmarks Register and on the National Register of Historic Places.

The cemetery is a private graveyard for the residents of Smithfield and the Isle of Wight County. The land it is on had been part of the T. B. Wright farm until it had been laid out along the slopes of ground overlooking the Pagan River. It has been the burial grounds for many of the area's prominent citizens, like Joel Holleman (1799-1844), who was the Speaker at the Virginia House of Delegates and had also served in the Virginia Senate and the U.S. House of Representatives. Others buried here include Pembroke Decatur Gwaltney Sr. and his son, Pembroke Decatur Gwaltney Jr. (Sr, the peanut industry pioneer and Jr. the pork industry pioneer), Parke Shepherd Rouse Jr. (1915- 1997), who was a newspaperman, author, historian, and Virginia Laureate, 1988, Hardy Cross (1885-1959), American Engineer, and John W. Lawson (1837-1905), physician, farmer, and who served in the U.S House of Representatives, Virginia House of Delegates and Virginia Senate.

This cemetery's landscape design follows the natural contours of the land, including wooded areas and rolling hills. It was situated well away from urban development.

Sallie Minton's gravestone

THE AUTHOR'S VISIT AND INVESTIGATION OCTOBER 23, 2019

My husband and I drove down to Smithfield on October 23, 2019, as I had a few places left to check out. Bill took three days off, so we had plenty of time.

We thought we would get St. Luke's Historic Church tour done (I'd gotten it at a two-for-one price on Groupon), but they had a production company filming something that day in the church, so we said we would be back the next day and headed to Ivy Hill Cemetery. We drove down the main street that led to Historic downtown Smithfield, turning left onto another, and eventually coming to the road, where another left turn led us to the cemetery grounds.

Bill drove the car past the gates onto a gravel road, stopping to let me out, with specific paranormal equipment of mine, and my camera hung around my neck. It was a warm day and Bill drove along the road until he found a spot where he could park. I roamed among the graves, before heading over to the in-ground cremation. I snapped pictures along the way, using both my camera and my Smartphone, too. The in-ground cremation had 2018 on its sign.

There was a sign posted at the cemetery gates, stating that the Board of Directors was dedicated to keeping the grounds clean and beautiful. They wanted the visitors to follow the rules on the sign and help make the maintenance of the grounds as easy as possible.

I saw a few names repeated, families that obviously settled the place and their descendants. Cofer, Jones, Gwaltney, Todd, Young, along with many others buried there.

THE AUTHOR'S EVP AND GHOST BOX SESSIONS OCTOBER 23, 2019

I turned on the ghost box and asked, "Who had been cremated and had their ashes added to the spot?"

I didn't get an answer, so I assumed no one was put there yet.

I moved among the various graves, calling out last names of families buried there that I saw, hoping for responses.

"I see Cofer. Am I pronouncing it right? Any member of the Cofer families here? Say your last name, Cofer, if you are."

"There is a Ray Parker MD. A doctor. What kind of doctor?"

He didn't answer. Instead, my ghost box was turned off, meaning either there were spirits there, sucking the energy from the batteries, or they just turned it off. I got it scanning again, asking them not to use the batteries, but me, and use the box's scanning waves to talk to me. Still, the box shut off. Again, I turned it back on.

I asked again, "Any of the Cofers here?" A male voice replied, "Yes."

Finally, not the radio stations, but a voice.

"I see some 'Jones' on tombstones here." Another male voice said, "Don't."

Don't say the Jones name? Did he want me to be quiet? "I'm passing so many people who passed away." "Wilson." Another male voice spoke from the ghost box.

Was he telling me his first or last name? I wish I had heard it live at the time, then I could have searched or pressed for more details.

I saw the last name, Gaye, on some stones, so I asked if any of them were here.

Just quiet.

Not getting an answer, I pressed, "Is anybody still here? Anybody?"

A male voice said quietly from the box. "Me."

"Gaye?"

"Me."

Okay, now, I'm getting somewhere.

I asked, "Any of the Confederate dead here?"
Another male voice said, "I am."

"James Dooley Jordan?" "Yes!"

"Anyone else?" "Mark."

"Mark, where are you buried?"

"Here." Not very helpful as there were so many graves surrounding me.

Suddenly, a female voice piped up from the box, "Me!" Her next word was spooky. "Dead."

After that, not much else, so I did an EVP session (I learned later I got nothing from this), and after shutting off the box, headed for the car, snapping more pictures of various gravestones along the way, until I reached the car and got in the passenger side.

Bill was hungry, so we headed for Smithfield Station to eat and left the cemetery, and its dead behind.

Cemeteries are the last place to be haunted, some claim. NOT! Sometimes, the dead can't rest, or maybe they like to make sure no one litters the graveyard too, just like the sign at the gate asks.

Peaceful scene of graves and a tree with autumn
leaves at Ivy Hill Cemetery.

HISTORIC ST. LUKE'S CHURCH AND CEMETERY

"Men fear death, as children fear to go into the dark
and as that natural fear in children is increased with
tales, so is the other."
~Francis Bacon

Historic St. Luke's Church, once known as the
Old Brick Church, or Newport Parish Church, is
the oldest historic church in Virginia and oldest
church in British North America of brick
construction. According to local tradition, the
people built the structure in 1632, but other
evidence points to a later date of 1682.

St. Luke's Historic Church

It is a Virginia Landmark, and its building, historical site, museum, and gift shop are located in the unincorporated community of Benns Church, in Smithfield. The church museum is operated and owned by Historic St. Luke's Restoration, Inc, a fully-tax deductible, 501(c)3 non-profit organization.

Four generations of Virginians rest in the hallowed grounds of its cemetery. People can still purchase a cemetery plot for their burial here.

NOT GHOST STORIES

Not a ghost story, but something else: There's a tale from the late nineteenth century. A man on horseback went inside St. Luke's one night due to a heavy rainstorm. Suddenly, he heard a sound out in the adjacent cemetery. As he looked, he saw something colored white flapping around in an open grave. Heart pounding and chills running up his spine, the man leaped upon his horse and galloped out of there, thinking he'd seen a ghost or demon. The funny thing about this creature, the next morning, when the sun arose, they found a goose inside the pit. Frightened by the storm, it had fallen in and was just trying to escape. Proof that not every supernatural story or legend is caused by the dead.

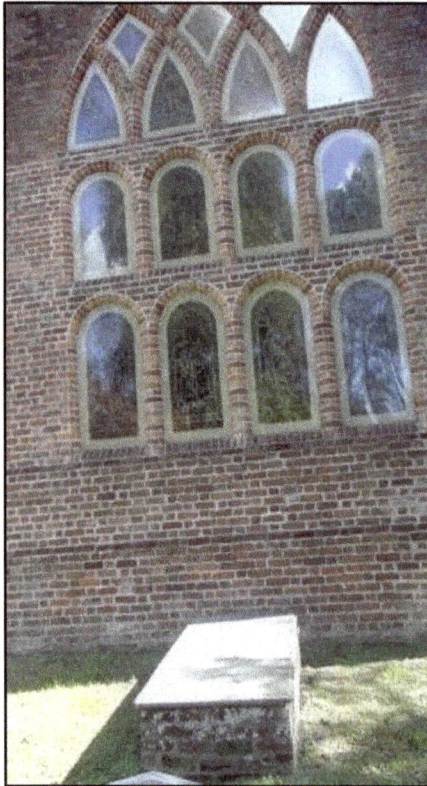

Reverend Alexander Norris's grave below the windows that he supposedly fell from in the ghost story.

Another non-paranormal story was told to me and others on the Historic St. Luke's Twilight Cemetery Tour on October 19, 2019. Our guide,

John, had stopped by a grave against the wall of the church building, at the back. He said that this was his favorite. The person buried beneath the slab was Reverend Alexander Norris, who died at age 39. Now, the folklore about how he became buried there is one night, he heard burglars in the church looking to steal the silverware, so he grabbed it and jumped up on the platform. Back then, the church windows were clear glass and could be opened out, so he fell out of the window and hit the ground, dying on impact. They buried him at that spot. It is said to this day, the ghosts of him and his horse haunt the place.

Is it true? No.

The true story happened to be he was coming back from Westover, where he was teaching African Americans to read and write, read their scriptures – something that was illegal in his lifetime and if he was caught, meant he could lose his freedom and be put in jail. He was coming back when he died from what they called in those days, Bilious Fever, which meant anything that swells your extremities. The writing on his tombstone saying he died here actually means he died in Smithfield.

I had asked if the folklore was told maybe to cover up what he had been doing with the African Americans, but John said no, more likely some person who didn't know the history or the truth wanted to look big in his children's eyes, so he told the story as he believed. And over the years, like all stories, it took on a life of its own.

THE AUTHOR'S TWILIGHT CEMETERY TOUR
OCTOBER 19, 2019

What I learned on the website when I went to purchase my ticket online for the Historic St. Luke's Twilight Cemetery Tour: "Dead men don't tell tales, but their tombstones do! Historic St. Luke's Church has been the site of burials since the 1600's. Enjoy the stories of local saints and sinners on a 30-minute, family-friendly guided tour through the Ancient Cemetery." Of course, I bought the ticket! I mean, I would be traipsing among old tombstones that went as far back as the 1600s. Besides, a good chance for night pictures and maybe I might get EVPs on my recorder, besides the guide telling the stories.

I thought I would be the only person on the tour, as they'd called me about changing to an earlier one. But I was worried about making it for the earlier time as I had a book signing at Barnes and Noble in Short Pump that ended at five o'clock, and it would take two hours to get to St. Luke's, making me late for the seven o'clock tour. I asked if I could do the one at 8:00 p.m. They said yes, relieved not to have the 9:30 one, even if that still meant I would be the only one on the tour at eight. But some people came at the last minute and signed up, so it wasn't just me.

Our guide, John, told anyone who did not have a flashlight to take one of his, as it would be dark in the cemetery, except for a few lights. I had my own with me, and after turning on my audio recorder, I hung my camera straps around my neck. I followed the crowd. John took us to several gravesites, but I will touch on only a few. Those that sounded interesting and had great stories attached to them—like the members of the Jordan family that were buried in the cemetery.

An interesting fact was how they pronounced the name back then. They called it 'Jerdan', not Jordan. One story concerned a young Jordan boy, who stood up in church and said that Jesus was baptized in the River Jerdan. Was that true? John couldn't say for sure, but it was a cute story.

Another interesting gravestone was the one of Fanny Norris Parker. She died in 1866. Now she was a wealthy lady. How did John know? Most stones have the writing on the front, telling birthdates and when they died, even maybe "A Wonderful Mother," something like that. But Fanny had added writing on the back of her tombstone, too. It told about her funeral service, which meant the family had money, as they could afford etchings on both sides of the stone.

Below left, the front of Fanny's gravestone, taken during the Twilight Cemetery Tour, October 19, 2019
Below right, the back of Fanny's gravestone, taken during the daytime, so you can see the writing better.

John pointed out a small stone. It marked the grave of a three-year-old child. The writing on it said, "Little Boy Parker." Children that young who died did not have names given to them, because parents waited to see if they lived and if they had been born sickly. If the child did die, they gave the name they would have given them to the next child born. It was what happened back when people died from diseases that in today's modern world can be cured with a shot or medication.

Another bit of folklore I learned concerned a man named Blaney. He had many children, all of whom died young. He announced his land was cursed. Either no one would be able to have children, or if they did, those kids would die, just like all his had done. No one would buy his "cursed" land, until the Jordans bought it. Funny thing, they had four youngsters, all whom died under the age of ten. Did this prove the land was truly cursed? No, as John said, back then, people died from common illnesses, even accidents. The flu and other diseases treatable today killed you. A good reason to get that flu shot—right?

We also got to go inside the church. One of the oldest organs in the world was inside the building.

One of the oldest organs in the world in St. Luke's Historic Church

We were told to take a seat. John talked about one of the two graves embedded in the stone floor at the front of the church: Joseph Bridger, and the one beside him, which was not his wife, but Lady Anne, either his wife's sister or her aunt. Bridger was one of the wealthiest men in the New World. Initially, he was buried on his plantation, White Marsh, but his remains were taken from there as the land belonged to others in the 1990s, and they didn't take care of the family cemetery. He was also the man they came to when they wanted to build the church, being that he had the money to loan them. Bridger eventually owned 15,192 acres of land that included White Marsh, plus land in Surry and even in Maryland. He even served in the House of Burgess.

In 2007, forensic archeologists from the Smithsonian came to see if they could test Bridger's remains. That was when they discovered that the stone container his bones were in had been cut to fit the marble floor, not the other way around. Of course, they also learned much of his bones were not there. They even found a bone from livestock mixed with his! They did take some of the bones back to the Smithsonian to test and found the man had stood 6 feet, 2 inches—tall for his time. He also died from the wealthy man's cause of death back then, the dry gripe. In other words, he ate off and drank from dishes and cups made of pewter, getting what we might call lead poisoning today.

Right at this time, archeologists are searching on the White Marsh Plantation land for more of his remains, which they will give to St. Luke's. They'd especially like to find his facial bones, to see what he looked like, as his skull had not been in that stone box.

After the tour, we headed back to the Visitor's Center. But I went back out to the cemetery to snap some pictures.

Then, I joined Bill, and we went out to the car to head home.

THE AUTHOR'S DAYTIME HISTORIC ST. LUKE'S CHURCH TOUR OCTOBER 24, 2019

We got up around seven on Thursday, October 24th, and drove to the tour. It was a nice sunny day, and both of us were well-rested and ready to visit this place and Windsor Castle Park. We ended up doing Windsor first, then headed to St. Luke's.

After my paranormal investigation in the cemetery, I met Bill and our tour guide inside the Visitor Center. She took us from there to the church. She took a picture of us together in front of the church (and later inside, too), saying it would be nice for us. She began talking about the church—the door was a Wicket door, meaning a door within a door, and around the doorway and windows was Romanesque. The quoins (pronounced coins) and pediment was Jacobean. The Y trace windows were gothic. Eighty percent of the brick is original, and there has never been a bell in the bell tower. They just added that tower to make it look taller.

Inside there was a baptismal font, a sounding board in the days when the church was used as a church, and the Episcopalian priests didn't have microphones like priests and ministers today have.

There were two important dates for the building concerning restoration. A hurricane hit in 1887, damaging much of the building, as trees fell on it. So, they had to restore the church in 1890-94. The second time was in 1953 when the Richmond Diocese said they would no longer fund the church. That was when St. Luke's became an organization to do with history, and they had to get money from donations to perform another restoration on the church.

THE AUTHOR'S PARANORMAL INVESTIGATION OF THE CEMETERY OCTOBER 24, 2019

Since our tour of the church wouldn't start for another hour, I went out into the cemetery to do ghost box and EVP sessions, along with taking some daytime pictures. After I took the photos, I switched on the ghost box and began.

"Any spirits here?"

The box shut off. Was it due to entities already sucking at the batteries, or had some invisible hand turned it off? I went ahead and restarted it.

I saw the name Todd on some graves nearby and asked, "Are any of the Todds here?"

As I listened in the quiet of my house later, I heard two different voices answer, "Yes." One was male, the other female.

I asked if Eliza Todd was there but didn't receive any answer that I heard live or later on the recording.

I pressed on. "Did you go to church here?" "Yes."

I said, "Who still hangs around here?" Another voice: "Me."

"I see Nannie. A lot of Nannies are connected to the Todd name."

A man's voice spoke from the box that I heard again on the recording. "Todd."

"How many of the Todds are here right now?" A woman spoke. "10."

"Anyone else. Give me your name." Another woman said, "Beth."

I said I was going to ask something different. "What did you like to eat when you were alive?" "Bread," said a male voice. "Nuts," said a woman.

I had gotten other sounds or voices, but many were too low, even later listening to the recording, or static hid what they had said. But when I saw a veteran of the 1812 War (they had metal signs next to their gravestones) I inquired, "Is the War of 1812 veteran here with me?"

A man answered, "I am."

I thanked him, then told him I was shutting off the ghost box and trying an EVP session. I did this for fifteen minutes and got nothing except one "Yes" when asked if they went to St. Luke's Church when alive.

I conducted another ghost box session as I stood in front of the church. Remembering about Joseph Bridger and his grave inside the church, I asked a specific question.

"Is there anyone connected to Bacon's Rebellion with me right now?"

A man's deep voice spoke out loud and clear, so that I heard right then. "Yes."

"Are you the one now buried inside the church?"

"Yes."

Glancing at my watch, I realized I only had five minutes before the tour, so I said, "I am shutting off the box, so goodbye. Good day."

A woman's voice replied, "Good day."

FORT HUGER

"A ghost is someone who hasn't made it - in other
words, who died, and they don't know they're dead.
So, they keep walking around and thinking that you're
inhabiting their - let's say, their domain. So, they're
aggravated with you."
~Sylvia Browne

The Hot Shot Furnace and Shell House at Fort Huger

Fort Huger is a Civil War fort located on a bluff
that overlooks the James River in the northern
reaches of Isle of Wight County, off route 10 and 8
miles from downtown Smithfield. It, along with
Fort Boykin, had been established to block the
Union approach by land and river to the
Confederate capital in Richmond. Confederate
engineer Col. Andrew Talcott surveyed several
defensive sites on the James River in 1861. He

had done this to protect Harden's Bluff and nearby Fort Boykin, along with Richmond.

The site at Harden's Bluff was named Fort Huger for Gen. Benjamin Huger, who commanded the Department of Norfolk. Benjamin Huger was a career U.S. Army ordnance officer who fought with distinction during the Mexican-American War besides serving as a Confederate general during the Civil War.

A thousand hands of slaves and free blacks constructed the fort under the direction of the Confederate Engineer Bureau, besides detachments of Lt. Col. Fletcher Archer's 5th Virginia Infantry Battalion.

The fort is oddly shaped, as that was the natural, geological shape of Harden's Bluff. The fort was made to fit the highest point of Harden's Bluff. Belief is where the flagpole is today, is where they began to build the fort, moving the earth and flattening it as they went. When they got to the edge, they just built a wall. It is thought that the heavy cannons brought to the fort were brought over water, as it was more straightforward. Historians think they used a sand ramp, hauling the cannons in, destroying the ramp afterward.

Where you can see the James River Reserve Fleet, it would have been double that for the Confederates to fire at the Yankee boats on the river. Straight across the river from Huger is Mulberry Island, where another Confederate fort was located.

There is a crater, where the powder magazine had been, but it's unclear who blew it up.

No reconstruction has been done on the fort. What one sees is what has been there since early 1862 when the Confederates left. The guns here now are reproductions, but they are in the exact spots the originals were. Archeologists found rusted nails and spikes where platforms had been and put a cannon there to cover them up. There was also a house where shells were stored, which made it safer and more convenient to bring the fuses and shells here. There was also a shot furnace. Any fort, even ships back then, had these. Solid iron cannonballs were heated up red hot, then were loaded into the cannon with wet wadding and powder and then fired at a wooden ship. That hot cannonball would strike the wood and set fire to the vessel. That method became obsolete with the introduction of iron ships, of course.

Isle of Wight County restored and interpreted this fort in 2007. Tourists and locals can view the James River Reserve Fleet on the James River, take the self-guided walking tour through the new trails, and see the cannon mounted along the edges of the fort. It is family-friendly and wheelchair accessible. The park is fifty acres.

The Author's Paranormal Investigation of Fort Huger

Bill and I drove, letting the feminine voice on his phone's GPS led us to where Fort Huger was situated. He parked in the parking lot and left the AC on as it was hot. After spraying on bug spray and putting on sunscreen, I hung my camera by its strap around my neck, gathered my ghost box, my digital recorder, and my EMF meter, and took off. I stopped and read the first sign, snapping pictures of it for reading once I was home.

I began an EVP session at my first stop after taking some pictures. I asked the usual questions. For my last question, I asked them to rap on the sign or make some sound that I could hear with my own ears or on the recorder later and not mistake for something in the woods or on the graveled trail.

I turned on the ghost box with my recorder still running. "Is there anyone from the spirit world here at Fort Huger?"

A female voice chimed in. "Brett."

"Who's Brett?"

A male voice answered, "It's Brett." "Were you a Confederate soldier here?" I thought he said no.

To be sure I heard right, I asked, "Did I hear a no?"

"No."

All right. "Had anyone died here at the fort, during the War Between the States?"

Another male voice answered, "Yep." Another blurted out, "Fort."

I asked if they had died by cannon fire and receiving no answer, I asked if they had died by rifle. One male voice replied, "Yep."

I asked how many helped build Fort Huger. I got different male voices calling out, "Me!" I asked for names, but they kept saying me.

I thanked them for the answers and shut off the box and recorder, snapped a couple more photos, then headed back up the trail to the parking lot where Bill was waiting in the car. It felt good to crawl inside and let the air conditioning cool me down.

Fort Boykin Historic Park

"Why do men fight who were born to be brothers?"
~James Longstreet

Fort Boykin Historic Park has been a part of American history since 1623. At first, it was a fort known as the Castle, constructed to protect the Jamestown colonists from Native Americans and raiding Spaniards. It stood atop a bluff overlooking the James River—making it a keen observation point. It had been used in the Revolutionary War, War of 1812, and the Civil War. Today, it remains essentially intact and constitutes a well- preserved example of military architecture of the Civil War era. The fort is also listed on the National Register of Historic Places, Virginia Landmarks Register, Virginia Civil War Trails, Captain John Smith's Trail and the Star-Spangled Banner Geotrail.

Besides a wildlife and birding trail, it has the second oldest black walnut tree in the commonwealth. This tree is over 200 years old and named to the Remarkable Trees of Virginia Project. The park is part of the Cornell Bird System.

The gazebo where I did the ghost box and EVP sessions at Fort Boykin, it overlooks the James River.

GHOST STORIES

There are stories told of a Civil War soldier spotted near Fort Boykin and the rocks located on the banks of the James River. One paranormal group investigated the park, but they found nothing.

AUTHOR'S PARANORMAL INVESTIGATION OF FORT BOYKIN

Bill and I found Fort Boykin Park after doing Fort Huger, using the GPS, of course. At first there was only one other parked car there, but soon after our arrival, others came. The park has a beach, and I saw some people with towels and other items heading up the trail to that spot.

I hiked to a spot that overlooked the river and after turning on my recorder and placing it down, I snapped a few quick photos, then switched on my ghost box and went into a session.

"Anyone who fought in the War Between the States still haunting here?"

No answer.

"No soldiers here?" If so, give me a name." "Bob."

"Last name?" (They don't always give out complete names, but I had success before.)

"Bishop."

"Who's Bishop? You, Bob?"

"Were you in the infantry? Confederate Navy? Union Navy?"

A male voice from the ghost box said, "Ship."

"Yankee or Confederate?"

"Confederate."

Ah, now this was good.

"What did you eat while at Fort Boykin? Hardtack? Johnny cakes? Did you drink coffee? I drink coffee; in fact, people alive today drink coffee."

"Coffee."

"What year is this that you drank coffee?" Again, I got, "Coffee."

I asked if they died in battle or lived through the war and passed away later. No one replied to that.

I thanked them before shutting off the ghost box and went into an EVP session using my recorder. But my batteries died, and I had to head back to the car, to reload new ones and we left the park. I hoped I could return when it was cooler, as it was in the 90s and I had one more stop to make, Boykin's Tavern.

Whether you come to Fort Boykin's to check out the history, enjoy the beach and park, or do a paranormal investigation, be forewarned, the ghosts are still there guarding their fortifications—and maybe, enjoying a bit of spectral cup of coffee while perusing sunbathing, lovely ladies in bikinis. But don't blame them, after all, while alive, women wore gowns down to their feet and used parasols to keep the sun off their pale skin.

BOYKIN'S TAVERN

"As a child, I loved ghost stories."
~Rebecca Hall

Boykin's Tavern

Boykin's Tavern is named for Francis Boykin, who served as a lieutenant with Patrick Henry and later camped with George Washington at Valley Forge.

I did an EVP session first. The only voice I got off it said, "Yes," after I asked if any spirits were there.

I switched on the ghost box. By now, it was close to noon, and the sun was boiling down on me.

"Any spirits around Boykin Tavern?" "Yes," "Who said yes?"

"Me." The voice was male, sounding like a man and not a boy. I wish they would say their names and not 'me'.

"Is Mr. Boykin here?" Nothing.

"Anybody? Male, female spirits?" A feminine voice replied, "Yes." "Did you die in the house?"

The same female voice replied, "Yes."

"Were you here during the Civil War? Revolutionary War?"

Some words came across, but I couldn't make them out. I asked for a name and got this: "Pam."

That is creepy, as that is my name, but did she mean her name, or that she heard my name and was giving it to me?

Finally, I asked again if Boykin was there.

The female voice came from my box. "Boykin."

I went ahead and took some more pictures after I shut off the ghost box, but it had grown so hot that I decided to get in the car, and we drove off to find a dining spot for lunch.

History may be dead, but not at Boykin's Tavern. Even in 90-degree heat.

ALONG ROUTE 460 EASTBOUND

WAVERLY

"Without peanuts, it isn't a cocktail party."
~Julia Child

Maybe Waverly and Wakefield are in Sussex County, but you must pass through them on Route 460 to get to Ivor, Zuni, Windsor, and Suffolk. Sussex County is a rural county located in the Commonwealth of Virginia. The first commercial peanut crop in Virginia was grown in Sussex County (near what is now Waverly) in the early to mid-1840s.

Waverly is an incorporated town in Sussex County. You drive through it heading southeast on Route 460. It is the first town one finds after leaving Prince George County.

There is a story that William Mahone, builder of the Norfolk and Petersburg Railroad (which we now know as Norfolk Southern), traveled with his wife, Otelia Butler Mahone, along the newly completed Norfolk and Petersburg Railroad naming stations. Otelia was reading *Ivanhoe*, a book written by Sir Walter Scott, and they say that she chose the names of Waverly, as well as Windsor and Wakefield, from this novel. She also tapped the Scottish Clan of "McIvor" for the title of Ivor.

William Mahone became a Major General in the Confederate Army during the War Between the States, and a Senator in the United States Congress later in life. A large portion of U.S. Route 460 between Petersburg and Suffolk is named in his honor.

The first known commercial peanut crop of Virginia originated in Sussex County, near the present-day town of Waverly, in 1842. There is even a marker for it that you can see when driving down 460 South. And it has the first peanut museum in the United States, the Miles B. Carpenter Folk Art Museum. The first commercial peanut distribution company was located across the street from the museum. The Peanut Museum is open for the same hours as the Carpenter Museum and opens on appointments. They welcome groups to come in and listen to their fascinating stories about the peanut.

You can see more about the museum at milesbcarpentermuseum.com.

WAKEFIELD

Also located in Sussex County, is the town of Wakefield. Wakefield is an incorporated town in

Sussex County and is the home of the Virginia Diner ("Peanut Capital of the World"). It also has the National Weather Service Weather Forecast Office for Eastern Virginia, the Troxler Memorial Library, Wakefield Foundation, and Plantation Peanuts of Wakefield.

Virginia Diner

A WAKEFIELD GHOST STORY

"Belief is the uncritical acceptance of something you can't prove."
~Hans Holzer

One of the employees at the Smithfield Bakery told me a story about an old, haunted farmhouse she owns in Wakefield. She asked that her name not be used, but she did give me permission to write her tale in this book. The house had the ghost of a man who'd been hit by a vehicle as he rode his bicycle home from the grocery store.

Instead of heading to the other side of the veil, his spirit went to the house and stayed.

The bakery woman said her mother-in-law could never get anyone to come clean the house after the first couple of workers had run-ins with the ghost. As for her daughter-in- law, her golden retriever loved the phantom. The dog never freaked out like many pets do with the paranormal. But after time, the woman told the ghost he had to go on and leave the house. He must have taken her advice to heart, because after that, she never saw or heard him again.

TOWN OF WINDSOR

"Towns oftener swamp one than carry one out onto the big ocean of life."
~D. H. Lawrence

The Town of Windsor, located in southeast Virginia, with a population of 2,626, has been called "the hidden jewel of Western Tidewater." It is located on Route 460 just west of the City of Suffolk. The Isle of Wight County owns and operates the town's sewer system, although the town operates its own water system. The Isle of Wight school system serves the schools.

The first recorded name for what became the Town of Windsor was Corrowaugh. In 1852 Corrowaugh was established as a post office, and mail was brought once a week by courier until 1859 when the contract for mail service was given to the Norfolk & Petersburg Railroad (now

Norfolk Southern). The railroad built a depot, and it was called Windsor Station. In 1902 some of the citizens decided it was time to organize the town. The charter was Postmaster granted by the General Assembly on March 15, 1902, and Windsor Station became the Town of Windsor, Virginia.

A WINDSOR GHOST STORY

There are claims of a house built in the 1930s in Windsor where a shadow person has been seen, along with tapping on the windows heard and lights blinking. I haven't found anything else to prove or disprove this tale.

SUFFOLK

"I have never felt salvation in nature. I love cities above all."
~Michelangelo

Suffolk is in the Hampton Roads metropolitan area, and it is the largest city by area in Virginia. The city had a total population of 84,585 at the time of the 2010 census.

Planters Peanut Center

Indigenous tribes lived in the region for thousands of years. When the English settled in Jamestown, the Nansemond Indians lived along the river. In the early colonial years, the English cultivated tobacco as a commodity crop but later turned to mixed farming, which some used enslaved Africans.

Founded by English colonists in 1742 as a port town on the Nansemond River in the Virginia Colony, Suffolk was known initially as Constant's Warehouse, for John Constant, but was renamed after Royal Governor William Gooch's home of Suffolk County in East Anglia in England.

Suffolk became a land transportation gateway to the areas east of it in South Hampton Roads early in its history. Both the Portsmouth and

Roanoke Railroad and the Norfolk and Petersburg Railroad were built, and they passed through Suffolk, early predecessors of 21st century Class 1 railroads operated by CSX Transportation and Norfolk Southern, respectively. All this happened before the American Civil War. Other railroads and later major highways followed not long after the war.

A hundred years ago from 2016, Mr. Peanut, who we see as the mascot on Planters Peanut jars and cans today, was born in Suffolk. A young boy, Antonio Gentile, created the original drawing soon adopted by Planters Peanuts.

Peanuts symbolize mystery since their shells hid their contents entirely. Called "treasures beneath the ground," nuts are also associated with wisdom because their contents are compact, sustaining, and enclosed within a single shell. Long ago, peanuts were wrapped in gold or silver foil and used as Christmas tree ornaments.

Each year in October, Suffolk holds the Suffolk Peanut Fest, which is a county fair for the city, in honor of the peanut. The city holds the Suffolk Peanut Fest Parade in downtown Suffolk and the following weekend is the festival itself, with amusement rides and games, festival food, hot wing eating contest, a demolition derby, entertainment, an arts and crafts exhibit, bingo, monster truck rides, petting zoo, peanut butter sculpting contest, activities especially for children and seniors, and much, much more. I couldn't attend this year's festival myself, as I had Monster Fest October 5th, and the following Saturday, the Yorktown Fall Festival. You can check when the festival will be held in 2020 and beyond at their website, www.suffolkpeanutfest.com.

The city has a ghost tour, too. If you take this tour, be sure to wear comfortable walking shoes as you will be walking through quite a bit of historic Downtown and on your way back through the Cedar Hill Cemetery to return to the Suffolk Visitor Center. It is a very cool way to get in your exercise and learn some haunting stories about various places.

Nansemond County Courthouse (Suffolk Visitor's Center)

RIDDICK'S FOLLY HOUSE MUSEUM

"Within, walls continued upright, bricks met neatly, floors were firm, and doors were sensibly shut; silence lay steadily against the wood and stone of Hill House, and whatever walked there, walked alone."
~Shirley Jackson

Riddick's Folly House Museum

Riddick's Folly is a historic house built in Suffolk in 1837, and is made up of four floors, twenty-one rooms, and sixteen fireplaces. All four stories in the house are open to the public. Mills Riddick built the house. Mills' contemporaries soon ridiculed the house and labeled the building "Riddick's Folly" due to its enormous size and its avant-garde Greek Revival architecture. The structure's distinctive design features Flemish gables, five eyebrow windows just below the eaves, and interior carved cypress woodwork.

Mills was a member of a prominent family of Suffolk and Nansemond County, a grandson of Revolutionary War hero, Colonel Willis S. Riddick. Besides a cavalry captain during the War of 1812, Mills also represented Suffolk and Nansemond County in the Virginia House of Delegates in 1819 and 1829.With his death in 1944, his son, Nathaniel, inherited the house and lived there with his wife, Missouri, and their five children. Nathaniel was a lawyer, later a judge, and was also a member of the Virginia Legislature. His oldest child, Anna Mary, was the first child born at Riddick's Folly, with her birth being July 21, 1841. Anna Mary's siblings were Mills Edward, John Thompson, Missouri Taylor, and twins Nathaniel Henley and Cordelia Kilby. Cordelia Kilby died at birth. As a young lady, Anna Mary attended Hayden Hall in Smithfield. She also attended Norfolk Female Institute. Anna Mary loved to read and sew, was a talented artist, and an accomplished pianist, too. Some of her paintings still hang in the museum today, and I can attest, they show how talented she was. After the Civil War, Anna Mary and her sister Missouri (Zouzie) felt determined to restore Suffolk to its former glory.

They also sought to help those families affected by the War Between the States. The two sisters started the Mite or Ladies Aid Society; they also founded the Randolph Society of St. Paul's Episcopal Church. Anna Mary became a charter member and became president of the Suffolk Chapter of the Daughters of the Confederacy for

30 years. She was a charter member of the Association for the Preservation of Virginia Antiquities, King's Daughters, Daughters of the American Revolution, and even a member of the Suffolk Literacy Club. She was the first woman to vote in Suffolk. Anna Mary never married and lived in Riddick's Folly until her death on November 11, 1936.

The family fled to Petersburg when the Union occupied Suffolk; the house became headquarters for General John J. Peck and his staff of Army officers. The house was simultaneously used as a hospital for sick and wounded Union soldiers. Many of the penciled messages and autographs written on the walls by those soldiers have been carefully preserved and are still legible today on the top floor. The room is still set up as it might have been during the occupation, with a desk like Peck might have used, a bed, and more, including a soldier's wooden leg. The family returned three years later and found their home stripped of most of their possessions. Riddick's descendants continued to live in the home until 1967.

Nansemond County purchased the house and grounds for use as office space. In 1977, Riddick's Folly became a facility for cultural events in Suffolk. In 1988 and 1989, the house underwent an extensive, privately funded restoration. It became Suffolk's only house museum. The place has kept up the acquisition of period furnishings, ongoing research, and further restoration.

Riddick Graves at Oak Hill Cemetery in Suffolk

THE AUTHOR'S VISIT AND THE GHOST STORIES

Bill and I took a tour of the house on the afternoon of Friday, August 12, 2016. We learned that the rug on the first floor was painted and not a real woven rug. You couldn't tell. There is a newly remodeled gift shop in the English basement—that was once Riddick's Folly's larder room or pantry. The basement also contained the dining room, the winter kitchen (the summer kitchen would have been outdoors), laundry, and the room where the slaves who did the cooking and laundry lived.

The first floor has the doubled parlors where the ladies and gentlemen met with other ladies for tea or knitting, and men to talk politics and business, where it can be opened up for dancing at parties. Rooms to the left of the hall, one was a gentlemen's library, while the other used by Anna Mary as a ladies' parlor. The latter was used by Mills during the last five years of his life, as he was not in the best of health, until he passed away in it.

The second floor was where the parents' and adults' bedrooms were. This floor was plain, more every day than the first floor where the family entertained their visitors.

Riddick's Folly has two permanent exhibit galleries on its third or topmost floor. They are "Our Bleeding Country" and The Mills E. Godwin, Jr. Gallery and Research Library. "Our Bleeding Country" examines the Civil War's impact on the Suffolk community. The Mills E. Godwin, Jr. Gallery and Research Library is about the life of one of Virginia's governors. The children had their bedrooms up there, along with the nannies and slaves/servants who took care of them. The room with the soldiers' signatures was on that floor. Our guide told us how back in the seventies, some local teachers had come in with cleaning supplies and began to try and clean off the writing on the wall, thinking it was graffiti. Luckily for future tourists, they were stopped before history was wiped away, and the writing covered over with see-through plastic to protect it from then on. There is a bloodstain on the floor in the room that no one has been able to clean off. When the lady docent who took our tour fee in the gift shop discovered I was there to find out if the house was haunted, she told me to come back the next day and talk to Edward L. King. I arranged to return at 2:00 p.m. the next day, August 13th, after my event, the New Authors Expo at the Suffolk Mystery Authors Festival ended at 1:00. She told me to use the back door to come inside the house, as it would be unlocked. Those who took the tour used the front door, but everybody else always used the back entrance.

The next day, at 1:30 p.m., Bill drove me to my interview with Edward L. King at Riddick's Folly House Museum. The day had grown hotter and was, in fact, the hottest day since summer began. I opened the back door and walked in, while Bill remained in the car, the engine running and the air conditioning on to keep him cool. I recognized the first floor of the house. Mr. King came out of a room to greet me and led me inside as he used it as his office, closing the door after I stepped inside. He sat down behind a desk while I seated myself in a chair in front of the desk. I realized this was the room Anna Mary used, and Mills was in when he was ill until he died five years later.

I asked him for stories about any paranormal activity in the Folly House.

He replied, "One paranormal group we had here one time told me they had sat on the floor in the parlor on the first floor. There was a tea set on a table in the room." This set was the same one the young guide we had the other day had shown to us. "Suddenly, a spoon that had been placed upside down in a cup, flipped across the room. Everyone in the group heard a voice after that, asking, "Who are you and what do you want?"

"Another paranormal group had gone up to the top floor and in the doorway of the room with the Civil War exhibit they saw a Confederate soldier standing there. The spirit knelt on the floor and then got back up."

King didn't know if they had gotten it on video or not.

He also told me a story concerning his late wife who passed away in January 2016. He had gone all the way downstairs to the basement while she vacuumed the third floor. She heard a noise from the first floor and thinking it must be her husband, she called out, "You can come up now. I'm all done."

Someone said from the first floor, "I'll be up."

It wasn't King, for he was still in the basement at the time.

King went on to tell me another story about visitors that came to the house before it was a museum. They were there to determine what needed to be restored and had just gotten to the fourth floor when suddenly, they heard loud, heavy footsteps above them.

One person asked, "Is there a floor above us?"

Another replied, "No other floor, just a small crawlspace between this last floor and the roof."

Mr. King told me that the crawlspace was in no way big enough for any living person to be able to walk upright inside of it. And no way could anyone walk on the roof.

Another time, when he had to come to the house, his wife remained in the car while he ran in. She could see the window of the Civil War exhibit room and at that time the room had no power. And yet, she saw a light going around in circles, as if someone carried it.

Another paranormal group told him they heard whispering coming out of the laundry room and heading into the kitchen—captured on audio. They also heard a woman's voice in the laundry room while in the basement, besides a woman humming in the gift shop. Could these be the slaves the Riddicks had? Whatever the case may be, Mr. King told me that all the paranormal groups they had investigate the museum felt the basement to be the most haunted spot in the house.

Another story about the ghosts he told me concerned the emergency lights in the hallway. One day they came on, even though the regular power was still on. No one could find any reason why this happened.

King played for me some files he had on his desktop computer. They have been given to him from several paranormal groups that had investigated the building. There was something on all three—too low for me to understand what was being said.

"Another time," said King, "I heard a door slamming hard. There are three exit doors. One is in the basement, but the sound did not come from down there. I rushed out, but found no one inside the house, or even outside."

At that moment, he was interrupted by his phone ringing. It was someone who'd brought him a twelve-foot ladder he had needed. So, he excused himself and left the room, closing the door behind him. I decided this would be as good a time as any for an EVP session.

I said, "I have two meters here - my regular EMF meter and another that has a blue LED light. You can use both to let me know you're here, or to answer me with the lights. I also have my recorder I used for interviewing Mr. King. You can talk into it."

"Give me your name. My name is Pam. What is yours?" "Is the lady of the house with me?" Later, as I listened at home a week-and-a-half later, I heard a feminine voice, very low. But at that time, I only heard murmurs from King and the person who brought the ladder, also male, outside of the room, in the hall.

"How many spirits are in the house?"

The EMF meter flashed at that moment. Though later, I didn't hear an answer on the recorder.

I said, "So, you are here. Do you like Mr. King? He's a nice man."

"What kind of food did you like to eat when alive?" "Can you make something in here move for me? Who flipped that spoon off the teacup and across the room for the group that one time? Can you give me a name? If you need help to answer, you can use my energy to help you."

Just then, Mr. King returned to the room as the other person had left. Both meters flashed as he sat down. I laughed. He thought he'd caused the effect, by touching the one meter. I told him to touch it again and he did, but the lights did not come on.

He said, "Mills Riddick, who built the house, died in this room. It was actually a ladies' parlor, but he spent his last five years in here, dying in it.

Samuel Riddick died in his law office in 1882. His body lay in the parlor for two weeks."

No doubt for a wake. Back then, those that died lay out in the parlors, as there were no funeral homes, or not many when the first ones were built.

As for the lady of the house, Anna Mary, she had a bed moved to another room. She lay in it, moaning, "I lost my family, I lost my friends, it is time for me to die." Just before she really did pass away, she said with venom, "I hate the Yankees!"

He also mentioned one recording done by a paranormal group on the top floor, when they asked for her, they got "Anna."

I asked if there had been anything paranormal experienced by him or anyone in his office. King said no. I told him I would do a short session with my ghost box.

There had never been a ghost box session done in the room before. I told the ghosts to use my energy to enable them to speak through the box, by way of the radio waves. I listened later as I also recorded the session for anything too low for me to hear or something I wasn't sure I heard in the moment.

As the scanning began, I asked, "Are you here, Anna Mary?"

No answer.

I tried again. "Anybody here with us?"

A man said, "Me." A woman said, "Me." Mills? Anna Mary?

"Can you tell me your name?" "No." This was a male voice. "Why not?"

I did not get an answer to that question. "You do know Mr. King here?"

A woman's voice issued from the box, but all I heard was: "We" ... the rest was too low, as I listened through my headphones later at home.

"Any of the Riddicks here?"

I heard both a woman's and a man's voice, but both too low to be audible.

"Mills, are you here?"

Two male voices replied, "Here," loud and clear enough to be heard by our own ears at the time. The second voice was deeper.

"So, you are here? Please, Sir." A man replied, "Yes."

"What about the lady of the house, Anna Mary?" Nothing.

"Are you listening to us?"

The scanning shut off. I assumed either they were sucking the battery power, or had turned off the scanning themselves, maybe tired of the questions. I went ahead and shut off the box.

King told me about a cover of Anna's. He had taken it out, but someone told him that maybe he shouldn't keep it out, so he put it away in a trunk. When he went to get it out for a second time, it was not inside the trunk. Nowhere at all. Later, he found it back in the trunk. Maybe Anna did not want it out.

Another time all the phones in the house did not work.

Nothing amiss with them, either.

As I listened to the interview on my laptop, after his story about the phones, four beeps sounded from my recorder. I knew I would need to contact King—I don't remember hearing the sounds live at the time.

This was when King told me about the group he was with that got together to honor another Confederate soldier at the Confederate Soldier Memorial in Oak Hill Cemetery. You can read that story in the Oak Hill Cemetery chapter.

At that moment, a sharp ping echoed from his desk between me and him.

"I heard a noise."

King said, "I heard a tone."

The recorder did capture it. I thought it sounded like the ring of a tiny bell. No reason for the resonance, nothing on his desk, my recorder only records and doesn't make any noises, my ghost box was shut off, and neither of the meters makes any sounds. Is someone trying to get our attention?

I asked, "Are you listening to us?"

Just then, the lights flashed on the meters.

Done with the interview and needing to get back to the Suffolk Mystery Authors Festival, I shut of the recorder and put it and the other equipment back into my bag. I stood, and King walked me from his office to the back door. He put his hand on the doorknob and twisted to turn it.

He turned to me and flashed me a shocked look, saying, "The door's locked!"

He had left the door unlocked after his visitor came with the ladder. In fact, he always left the back door unlocked and the front one, too, because of those coming in for a tour.

"Looks like they don't want me to leave," I joked. I looked around. "Thanks, but I need to leave, although your house is lovely."

King unlocked the door and opened it. I walked outside.

Later, on our way back home after the post-festival dinner for the authors and the volunteers, Bill stopped at the house for me to take some pictures, but looking over them the next day, I didn't find anything staring out of the windows. Nothing out of the ordinary.

Remember, don't agree out loud that Riddick's Folly House is a folly when you are taking a tour there. The ghost of Anna Mary may be listening, and she won't be pleased, and you may find the door slammed shut after exiting. But praise the place, and you may find yourself locked in, as they want you to stay.

PRENTIS HOUSE

"Ghosts could walk freely tonight, without fear of the disbelief of men; for this night was haunted, and it would be an insensitive man who did not know it."
~John Steinbeck

It is widely rumored to be the most haunted home in Suffolk. It was once the Suffolk Visitor Center until they moved to the Nansemond Courthouse. When I took the Suffolk Ghost Tour a couple of years ago in November, they talked about how it is considered the most haunted spot in historic downtown Suffolk.

The Prentis House

Footsteps and voices had been heard there when the Visitor Center occupied the building, and shadows were seen. Through a Suffolk News-Herald newspaper article back in 2011, when the building housed the Visitor Center, the tourism employees talked about hearing many footsteps at once walking around, lights coming on and going off by themselves, the door locking from inside many times, and even once, the remote control flying across the room. The Prentis House was the only building given the 'Haunted" rating by the Old Dominion University Ghost Hunters Club. This organization had recorded footsteps, humming, whispers, singing, and even a piano, when they investigated there.

Although no one has ever truly explained who or what is haunting the place, it was thought that maybe children, due to all the running up and down the stairs.

AUTHOR'S GHOST BOX SESSION OUTSIDE THE PRENTIS HOUSE

I crossed the street and headed over to the Prentis House to snap some pictures and do a ghost box session. It was chilly and windy, and vehicles sped down the road. I turned on my box and began.

"Are there any spirits inside the Prentis House?" A woman answered through the box. "Yes."

I asked, "Why are you haunting there?" No answer.

"How many spirits are inside the house?"

"10."

I didn't hear it completely, until later at home on my laptop. I also heard ten used again.

"Any female spirits?"

No answer.

"Any male spirits?"

"Sure." It was a man's voice.

"Name?"

"Tim."

It sounded like Tim to me.

"Did you live here? Is that why you haunt it?"

"No."

"Any from the Civil War?"

No answer, so I assume not, or they didn't want to answer that.

"So, you haunt the lawyers and the others that work in the offices in Prentis House?"

"Yes."

"Do they pay attention to you when you do?"

"No."

That was all I got as the cars speeding past grew worse, and the wind didn't help. I shut off the box, saying good-bye.

If you have a business and you'd like to rent an office at the Prentis House, just a warning, you might find yourself sharing the space with someone dead.

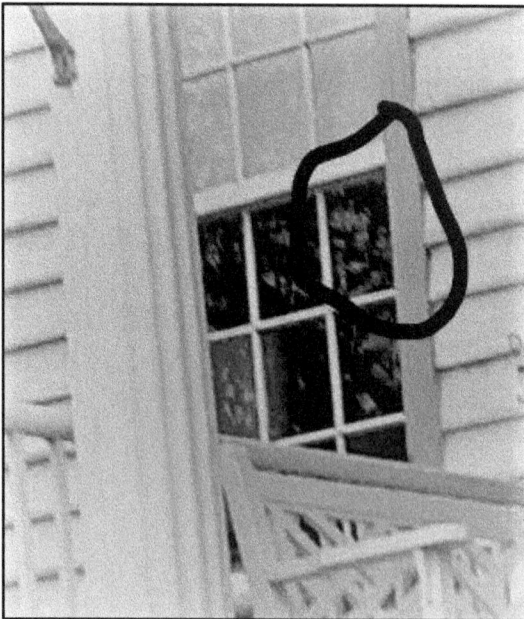

Face in Window of Prentis House-First Floor, taken
November 17, 2019. It wasn't in other photos taken of
the window, just clear glass.

BARON'S PUB

"Halloween isn't the only time for ghosts and ghost
stories. In Victorian Britain, spooky winter's tales were
part of the Christmas season, often told after dinner,
over port or coffee."
~Michael Dirda

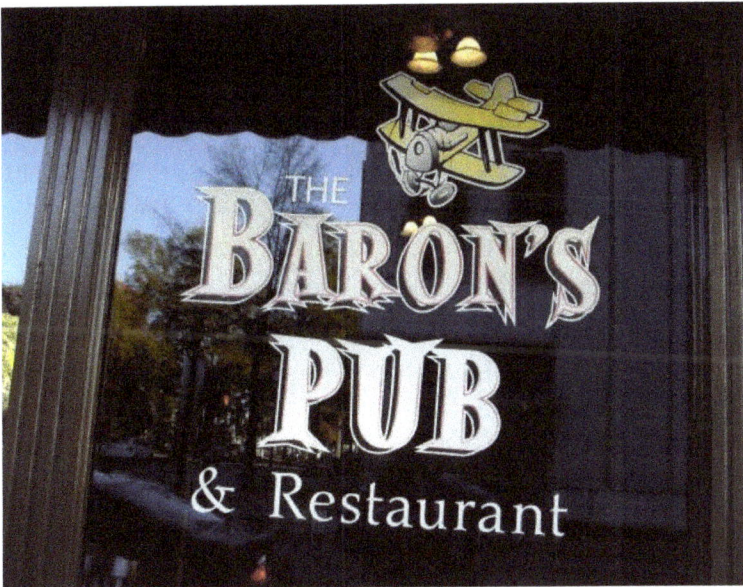

Baron's Pub sign

Baron's Pub is a restaurant and pub farther
downtown, outside of what most consider the
historic area of Suffolk. It is part of a tall building
that began as the Elliot Hotel in the 1920s.
Several residents of the Suffolk Towers apartment

building above the restaurant and pub have reported being disturbed by invisible, yet unruly, hotel guests who are still refusing to check out.

INTERVIEWING THE OWNER OF BARON'S PUB

I interviewed the owner of the pub, Mike Williams, plus I used my EMF meter to see what might happen as my husband and I ate dinner there on November 12, 2016. We talked about the hauntings there and even in the apartments above.

Mike talked about the man they caught on the security cameras. You could see the silhouette on the camera's monitor. He had sent it to the *Ghost Hunters* when the show was still on Syfy, but they were in their last year, and he has never heard back from them or had his DVD returned. I offered *Paranormal World Seekers* to investigate for him and film it for an episode of our show, promising him a copy of the DVD.

Some of the stories he told concerned the apartments. One man kept seeing a woman dressed in the Flapper style of the Twenties in his bathroom. People would hear footsteps in the hallway of the apartment building, with no one there. There were disembodied voices heard, plus specters seen.

As for his business, he would be awakened by the police when his alarm would go off, and he would have to drive there to shut it off. Funny thing, this always happened around four o'clock in the morning. "Finally," he told me, "I just said heck with it. I have insurance if it really is a fire or I'm being robbed."

The exciting thing about this was when we investigated the restaurant and pub for PWS, the alarm went off close to five in the morning when my co-producer Mark Layne walked out the side door, which had been disabled from the alarm so we could leave when done. I will tell more about that later when I talk about the investigation.

A couple of other stories not connected to his business or the apartments concerned Michi's Café. Long ago, it had been a mortuary where soldiers were brought in to be prepped (I am assuming these were Confederate soldiers and the time was the Civil War). Two or three apartments above the café, a woman was brushing her teeth when she saw a man in uniform in the reflection of her mirror.

After that, he had a waitress bring me his card for the future investigation. I turned on my EMF meter, and the recorder, to see what I could catch. I soon found that whatever spirit or spirits were in there, they liked to answer by the meter. Using it to confirm or say no, I learned male spirits were using it. As for the recorder, it was hard to tell, as there were people laughing and talking in the pub.

Baron's Pub on the rainy night where members of
Paranormal World Seekers and I did an overnight
investigation.

At some point during the investigation at Baron's Pub,
we all noticed that my co-producer's flashlight was on
and none of us had touched it.

THE INVESTIGATION OF BARON'S PUB JANUARY 2017

Mike did set up for us to investigate overnight on January 7, 2017. It was raining that night, but Bill and I drove to Mark Layne's production company office in Newport News. Carol Smith, my fellow investigator, drove her car and met us there too. After filming a brief piece of us talking about the upcoming investigation, we all drove to downtown Suffolk. We parked in the parking lot of the bank across the street from the pub. Still raining, I looked up at the building, up at where the apartments were and thought, *Looks creepy. Gothic.*

We had gotten there early to have a late dinner. The food tasted great, and it finally stopped raining, so Bill and Mark went to fetch Mark's filming equipment. I went ahead and did a ghost box session early down in the restaurant to see what we would get.

We did get one spirit who told us a few things. When I mentioned that my hand holding the ghost box was freezing, I asked if he was doing that.

His answer: "Hurt." I didn't hear this during the investigation, but after I'd arrived home the next day and uploaded the audio to my laptop, then listened by using my headphones. I rarely have any entity try to do any harm to me, but it felt obvious this one had tried.

I shut off the box and ended our conversation. I never got the impression he was there during the filming—maybe he stayed down in the part of the restaurant near the front door, or perhaps he left for the apartments?

I used a recorder for a camera Bill placed in the kitchen since the camera didn't capture sounds. Later, I listened to it and heard the clink of a glass being put down on metal, which I assumed would be the sink area. No one drank that night, and the kitchen staff had washed all the glasses and put them away before they left at 2 a.m. I also caught a low whisper, as if someone nearby had said something. It captured footsteps, too. Interestingly, the two people who were there to take pictures of what we were doing for the pub's website had mentioned hearing footsteps, as if someone walked from the bar into the kitchen. Although, the recorder wasn't placed in the kitchen until after they left.

Need a bite to eat. Well, Baron's Pub has great food and even a selection of beers and alcohol. Even more, they have ghosts!

The apartments above the restaurant have paranormal activity, too.

CEDAR HILL CEMETERY

"The popular notion that ghosts are likely to be seen in a graveyard is not borne out by psychical research... A haunting ghost usually haunts a place that a person lived in or frequented while alive... Only a gravedigger's ghost would be likely to haunt a graveyard."
~John Alexander

Cedar Hill Cemetery at night

Located at the corner of North Main Street and Constance Road in historic downtown Suffolk, Cedar Hill Cemetery is 32 acres of hilly terrain and cedar trees, a city-owned public cemetery dating back to 1802. It is also known as Green Hill Cemetery. Many veterans from World War I, II, Korean War, and Vietnam War are buried here, plus it is also the final resting place for

Confederate generals and soldiers. It was added to the

U.S. National Register of Historic Places in 2006 and is on the U.S. Historic District and Virginia Landmark Register too.

Grave markers within the cemetery date from the early 19th century to the present day and this cemetery is a representative example of public cemetery planning and funerary artwork found in southeast Virginia and Suffolk. The contributing structures include the Darden (1938), Hosier, Hill (1933), and Brewer-Godwin mausoleums, and the contributing objects include the Confederate Monument (1889) and World War I Monument. The entrance off Mahan Street houses monuments and a cannon that serve as a memorial to the veterans from different wars, who now lie buried in the cemetery. Cedar Hill also is the final resting place for many prominent citizens of Suffolk as well as former city and state officials, such as former Governor Mills Godwin. Cedar Hill has the City's first scatter garden, which allows the scattering of ashes in place of burial. A wrought-iron fence surrounds this garden with benches and a memorial board located at each end.

This is the story Edward L. King, a docent at Riddick's Folly House Museum, told me about the Confederate soldier spirit on August 13, 2016, when I interviewed him about the house. He'd been with the group when they got together to honor another Confederate soldier at the Confederate soldier memorial in Cedar Hill Cemetery. The professional videographer caught a ghost on his video for the Confederate memorial service in Cedar Hill Cemetery in 1999. The videographer had been hired to videotape the service of James Jasper Phillips, who was born on January 23, 1832 and died February 11, 1906, as marked at his gravesite. The videographer had panned his camcorder at the crowd and never noticed he had captured something else near some of the graves. Later, those he gave the tape to told him they saw an apparition in the video. He went back over the video and saw the soldier standing, his fist or hand over his heart. There were a few comments beneath the video, saying that the spirit was holding his hat over his heart as a sign of respect from those days.

You can view this video at:

https://www.youtube.com/watch?v=3T7oW_mjFp8

It is not the original one as I had seen it, as the videographer edited it.

I went there to do a ghost box session and see if anyone was still haunting the cemetery. I did get a male voice saying "Riddick" a couple of times, one time near their graves, and "We are still here."

I asked, "Who is all here?" They never answered me.

I snapped this photo of the King tombstone at Cedar Hill Cemetery when we came through the place on the last leg of the Suffolk Ghost Tour in November.

I captured paranormal mist during the Suffolk Ghost Tour.

OTHER GHOST STORIES OF SUFFOLK

LOCAL GHOST STORIES TOLD BY EDWARD KING OF RIDDICK'S FOLLY

"It's okay, if you don't want to believe in ghosts. It doesn't change anything. They still believe in you."
~Jason Medina

Edward King told me other ghost stories of the Suffolk area. One concerned the Princess (Preston) House where a stapler flew across a room that was used as an office.

The second story happened in a house on the other side of the train tracks down the road in the historic area. A worker was working in the basement and put down his tools. When he came back for them, they were not there or anywhere else in the basement.

The last story he told me could be taken with a grain of salt. He thought it could be in the Pepsi-Cola plant, but he wasn't sure. A woman was lying in bed when movement on her mattress woke her up. She sat up to find a Confederate soldier sitting on the edge of the bed.

MORE SUFFOLK GHOST STORIES

The story went that a couple lived in a house on White Marsh Road. They had a closet that had a light that often turned on by itself. They would pass by it, notice the light on, and turn it off. The next time someone went by it, the light would be on again. When the owners examined a photo they had taken of one of the windows, they saw a boy's face looking out of it. The boy did not live with them. When the closet was remodeled and they tore down the barn on their land, the ghostly boy seemed to disappear. One other time, as they got ready for bed, they heard what sounded like a party in the garage, with music and many voices. The husband grabbed his gun and rushed to the garage to see who was in there, but when he opened the garage door, nothing but silence met him, and he didn't see anyone.

Another story concerned a banshee. The hearing- impaired parents of Valerie Carver lived in Suffolk. The man was deaf, so when he heard the shrill scream of a woman at 4:05 a.m., he was shocked. Later that day, he received a call from a hospital his brother was admitted to after he had a stroke. His brother died precisely at the time he heard the scream. The next three nights, he kept hearing the same cry at the same time, until they buried his brother. Could this have been a banshee, and how was it able to penetrate the man's deafness, allowing him to hear? For after that, he no longer heard a sound.

Another woman used to live in an old house on Route 13 in Suffolk that people had told her had been used as a Confederate hospital during the Civil War. One day, her son came running down the stairs. He said that he kept hearing someone knocking on his door, but when he opened the door, he found no one there. It happened a few times before he freaked out and bolted from his room.

Their family had worked on the house for two months before they moved in, finding it peaceful at the time. After moving in, that all changed. They heard banging on walls. Their son and his friends saw a Confederate soldier. The spirit told them his name was Eddie. The kids claimed they could feel the ghost passing through their bodies on the first night when they didn't see him, and it scared them enough that their son's buddies no longer would come over.

At one point, they began hearing moaning coming through the speakers of their stereo. The family bolted from the home and stayed at the woman's mother's place. They told her what had been happening. They stayed at Mom's overnight and returned home the next day. There hadn't been any other activity since. Had the soldier been upset at their fear and just left?

INVESTIGATION OF THE SUFFOLK SEABOARD STATION RAILROAD MUSEUM

I heard that the image of a ghostly Confederate soldier had been captured on a security camera at the museum. It doesn't help that the station is right near the Oak Hill Cemetery, where Civil War soldiers were laid to rest. We stopped by the museum on Sunday, November 17, 2019, and while Bill wandered around, looking at the exhibits, I talked to the docent sitting behind the desk. He admitted being a skeptic and never had any encounters.

Suffolk Seaboard Station Railroad Museum

So, I did what I do in such cases and stood outside of the building and did a ghost box session to see if I could get anything.

"Any spirits connected to the train depot museum?" No answer.

"Any spirits connected to Oak Hill Cemetery, that are still haunting here?"

"Yep." This came from a male voice from my ghost box.

"So, you come from Oak Hill?"

"Yes." "Yes." Two voices chimed in.

"Who is the Confederate soldier seen on the museum's security camera?"

No answer.

"Did you fight in the Civil War and die?"

"Battle..." I couldn't hear the rest of that.

"I thought I heard battle. What battles? Battlefield?"

Something was said, but indistinguishable. It didn't help that the wind was blowing.

I thanked the spirits for any answers I might have been given and said good-bye, shutting the box and recorder off.

SUFFOLK GHOST TOUR

We were told a story on the Legends of Main Street ghost tour in November 2017 about the Suffolk Female Institute for Young Ladies and Little Girls, a finishing school also known as the Finney Institute from the 1860s to early 1900s. The building still stands, and it is claimed to host a mischievous ghost in its basement.

Another tale is about the father who, while fetching a doctor to care for his ill son, slipped on the railroad tracks, and a train decapitated him. It is said they never found his head and his spirit still searches for his lost head by lantern light during the night.

There's even a story told by a tenant in a Main Street apartment, about an impish specter that appears to only enjoy music by Elton John and Madonna, by not shutting off the radio, only doing that with other music played, and on occasion, will grab a slice of pizza from pizza boxes. I guess death doesn't stop a craving for a good pizza! The building was once a Civil War field hospital for both Union and Confederate forces. Bone fragments have been found on the building property that might come from surgeries and amputations once performed there.

A stop at the Riddick Folly House Museum – at night it looks creepy

Across the street from the railroad museum is the Gardner Store (circa 1790) at 341 N. Main Street. It served as a store and a home since 1825. The site is associated with a 19th century murder. Over the years, occupants of the store have reported tools that were put away at night would be found scattered the next morning, while shelves were inexplicably removed from walls and even various kinds of items are seen flying across the room. Its tearoom in the place is situated where prisoners were held during the Civil War.

Another story concerned an old penny that the owner of the house found on the window. She gave it to the Suffolk Visitor Center since it was historical, but it vanished from their center and ended up back at the house where it had been before. I guess the ghost felt it belonged to the house.

They claim there's no story about the Nansemond Courthouse, but again, it is a courthouse where trials were set. Overlooking the Nansemond River, the structure is set in the Roman Revival with very tall Tuscan columns. Today, it's no longer used for court trials, instead, the Suffolk Visitor Center is in the building.

It is the third structure on this site since 1840 at the busy intersection of Main Street and Constance Road. Fires had destroyed two previous courthouse buildings. The first fire occurred in May 1779 during the Revolutionary War, when the British burned the town, and most of it was destroyed after thousands of barrels of turpentine and pitch caught fire in warehouses along the river. Then, "The Great Fire" destroyed both sides of Main Street from the north of Mahan Street to the courthouse on June 3, 1837.

Old courthouse records document the trial of a Suffolk pastor, imprisoned for the murder of a fellow pastor he'd threatened after a decomposed body was found floating in the Nansemond River. The ironic twist to this case was when the presumed murder victim reappeared years later. He had been living in North Carolina.

SPOOK LIGHT OF JACKSON ROAD

The "spook light" is an alleged light that has been sighted on Jackson Road in Suffolk. Sighted in late summer or early fall, people made calls about it back in 1951. Deputy Hurley Jones was one officer who had investigated the sightings back then and saw it for himself. He described it as resembling a single automobile headlamp headed straight towards him. Another policeman who saw it was Sergeant W. S. Damercon, saying it looked like the bright light of a train coming off the tracks.

Having been there myself, it's a stretch of road that starts out and ends with a few homes, but most of it is only bushes to one side and woods on the other. Though it was daytime, and my husband sat in our car next to me, that lonely section gave me an eerie feeling, especially as no cars roared down it while I took pictures. I could believe how anyone might imagine a ghostly light speeding down the road at night.

Some people claim to have seen it all their lives. One resident of Jackson Road, Jeston Reid, acknowledged that his father had seen it seventy-five years earlier than the 1951 occurrence.

Digging deep, it was found that the old Jackson and Whaleyville railroad ran past where Jackson Road is now. There is a legend that claims a flagman had been killed on the line in 1912. Many believe it is he who is responsible for the light. But others say that the "light" has been seen long before the flagman's death.

Stories about how he died often vary. One has him as a member of a crew that was on a train that derailed. He lost his head when the cars piled on top of one another. Another tale has him struck down when he tried to warn the engineer about an oak tree that had fallen across the tracks, caused by a storm. The last story has him as someone who tried to flag down a train in the fog as his child was seriously ill. The engineer failed to see him, and the man was decapitated.

Whatever the legend, it seems on Jackson Road, this phantom is doomed to wander the tracks forever, searching for his head.

Remember the next time you're in Suffolk for their ghost tour or the Planters Peanut Festival, or just to see the historical places, or stopping for a bite to eat, the phantoms of the town are just dying to meet you!

HAUNTS AND LEGENDS OF THE GREAT DISMAL SWAMP

"They made her a grave too cold and damp
For a soul so warm and true;
And she's gone to the Lake of the Dismal Swamp,
Where, all night long, by a fire-fly lamp,
She paddles her white canoe."
~Thomas Moore

The Great Dismal Swamp National Wildlife Refuge is the largest intact remnant of a vast habitat that once covered more than one million acres of southeastern Virginia and northeastern North Carolina. It is a beautiful geological reserve full of animal and plant life, administered by the U.S. Fish and Wildlife Service. It lies on the Virginia-North Carolina line, bordering Suffolk and Chesapeake along its northern limits. Now there are over 113,000 acres, forty miles long and fifteen miles wide. In the heart of the park is Lake

Drummond, named for a Colonial governor of North Carolina.

Great Dismal Swamp Wildlife Refuge Park Office

The refuge is contained within the intersections of Virginia Highway 58, North Carolina Highway 158, and U.S. Routes 32 and 17. The headquarters and main trailheads are located on the western boundary in Suffolk.

The swamp is usually at its driest from June to October. A few years ago, a fire happened, and although the woods no longer burned, it still smoldered beneath the waters. The park didn't allow anyone to drive down to the lake, and so, I never got to see it while at the park when I was working on *Haunted Virginia: Myths, Legends, and True Tales* for Schiffer Publishing in 2008. At that time, I could only hike by foot along the wooden trails the park had in the woods so visitors could get down to the lake.

The swamp supports a variety of mammals, such as otter, bat, raccoon, mink, gray and red fox, and gray squirrel. White-tailed deer are common, and although less often seen, American black bear and bobcat inhabit the area, too. The refuge provides a habitat for a variety of reptiles and amphibians. Three species of venomous snakes—cottonmouth, timber "canebrake" rattlesnake, and the more common copperhead—occur here, along with 18 non-venomous species. There are fifty-eight species of turtles, lizards, salamanders, frogs, and toads observed in the area.

There are those who say they have sighted the 8-foot diamondback rattlesnake and coral snakes in the area. Herpetologists dismiss the accounts, which add to the folklore of the swamp if nothing else.

Tales about escaped slaves in the swamp have been a part of local lore for centuries. Recent studies in the Great Dismal Swamp have uncovered archaeological evidence to confirm the presence of maroon colonies. The runaway slaves were called maroons, a word that comes from the French word marronage, meaning "to flee." Communities of maroons developed throughout the American South, especially in inaccessible swampy areas. They lived in secrecy, so that makes it hard to figure how many called the Great Dismal Swamp home. Recent studies suggest, maybe as many as fifty thousand lived in the swamp. They may have settled in areas of slightly higher elevation than the rest of the swamp, called "mesic islands." The people had built cabins and lived in them, farmed there, hunted wild turkey, deer, and other game, and foraged for edible plants. With the end of the Civil War, they no longer had to hide and came out, settling in the area and worked on the canal as shingle gatherers, or as farmers.

Visitors to the refuge can visit the newly constructed Underground Railroad Education Pavilion—built to tell the story of maroons in the swamp.

Numerous legends have arisen there: like the ones of lovers cursed to haunt the swamp forever. The area is said to be inhabited by dragons, spirits, ghouls, and other strange beings. There are myths of Indian maidens abducted by strange 'firebirds' and warriors battling to save them from these fiends. Eerie lights have been seen dancing among the trees, and scary sounds echoing at night bring heart-pounding terror.

Is it only the imagination, or is it the truth? Whatever the case may be, the Great Dismal Swamp is more than an ecological wonder; it's a fountain full of myths and legends, and yes, even has true hauntings and cryptids like the Sasquatch and more.

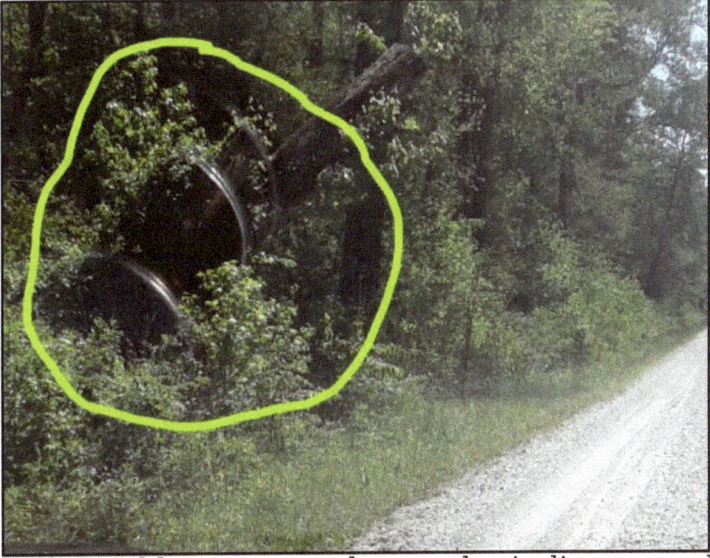

Weird possible paranormal anomaly circling around a tree at the Great Dismal Swamp, taken April 30, 2019

INDIAN MYTHS AND LEGENDS OF THE GREAT DISMAL SWAMP

CAUTAKA-THE HEALING POND

There is supposed to be a pond called Cautaka, or so the Native American tribes before the English came, believed. All the wounded or ill animals, big and small in Dismal Swamp, came to the pond to be healed. Some claimed they had been near it, but although they never found it, they would hear the wings of water birds or hear the bubbling water.

Those Indians who fasted or prayed during the night would receive visions of this pond. When dawn came, what they saw would include animals and birds splashing in it, even drinking from it, but when the morning became complete, the vision dissipated.

The natives say that after the English arrived, they caused the evaporation of the pond and cut down its purifying Juniper wood. And yet, they believed it was hard to destroy a miracle, and if you treat the beasts of the area with respect, one would have a good life. If one was lucky, one might encounter the brown waters of Cautaka.

FIRE BIRD

Two tribes of Native Americans once believed a fire bird lived in the swamp. Its eyes burned like flames, and when it flew over the trees, its fiery wings would singe their tops and cause them to burn. The hideous creature swooped down to snatch children and warriors in its beak, carrying them away to the center of the swamp.

These two tribes often battled, but when the fire bird settled in the heart of the swamp, they joined to fight it.

It was during one of their councils, a young brave named Big Bear fell in love with the beautiful maiden White Swan from the other tribe. She loved him, too, but she was already betrothed to the cruel and grizzled warrior of her tribe, Old Cold Heart.

Upset and wanting Big Bear, White Swan fled to the wilderness to seek out the Swamp Spirit for its help. The benevolent creature protected the swamp and those who lived in it.

She found the Swamp Spirit in the form of a gnarled old cypress that belched smoke and ash. Big Bear, who had followed White Swan unbeknownst to her, came out of the thickets to stand beside her. The lovers begged the spirit to find a way for them to be together, offering anything the spirit would want.

The Swamp Spirit demanded their first-born child.

Though shocked, White Swan and Big Bear agreed.

Suddenly, the fire bird appeared, as it had been watching them. The couple turned to run when they saw its flaming eyes, but the great bird snatched Big Bear in its beak and lifted him into the air.

White Swan, afraid for the man she loved, chased the bird deeper into the swamp, running as fast as she could.

The Swamp Spirit helped by lifting her into the sky, by changing her into a real swam so she could fly and catch up. The fire bird tried to smash Big Bear into a tree, but Big Bear tore himself loose from the bird's beak and fell right into the fire bird's giant nest. Made of the tendons and muscles of lost tribesmen, the scalps of warriors ringed the nest, while skulls and bones littered the ground below.

To Big Bear's horror, seven baby fire birds lunged at him, hungry for a meal. Their vicious beaks pecked at him, and their fiery wings singed his skin. While he fought to keep them from getting him, the adult fire bird went after White Swan in the sky.

Big Bear killed each of the young birds one by one. White Swan then appeared in the nest, and the voice of the Swamp Spirit spoke to them.

"Fire Bird knows that she cannot raise her young in the swamp as long as we have such brave Indians here."

Knowing it was defeated, the fire bird left the swamp, stopping only long enough to swoop down and grab Old Cold Heart from some hidden spot never divulged.

The legend claims that the bird left Old Cold Heart on a secluded island to live out the rest of his days. Or maybe he served as a delicious snack for an angry bird.

In the years that followed, water began to fill up the fire bird's nest. Native American lore tells that the nest formed Lake Drummond.

White Swan and Big Bear gave their firstborn to the Swamp Spirit, who turned the child into a white-tailed deer that protects the forest and leads hunters to safety.

How The Great Dismal Swamp Gave Away Its Poison

A plant grew in the shallow water of the swamp. Its vine was poisonous, and when the local tribes came to bathe in the water and touched it, they sickened and died.

The vine felt upset for killing anyone as it didn't want to do that, so it called the chiefs of the small inhabitants of the swamp to tell them it wished to give away its poison. These chiefs belonged to the wasps, bees, and snakes.

The wasp said, "I will take some of your poison, so I may be able to defend my nest. I will keep the poison in the tip of my tail, but I will buzz, warning those of what I intend to do."

Bee spoke up. "Give some to me for me to defend my hive. I will also buzz, warning people and animals. If I must use it, it will kill me as my stinger holding it will detach, which means I will be careful before using it."

Water Moccasin hissed, its tongue tasting the air. "I will take some, too, but only if people step on me. I will keep it in the fangs in my mouth, and I'll hiss and open my mouth, showing how white it is, so people will leave me alone."

The last creature, Rattlesnake lifted its head, shaking the rattle at the tip of its tail, and said, "I will take what you have left. I will keep it in my front fangs, and before I strike, I will shake the rattle at the tip of my tail. People and animals will know to watch for me and keep out of my way."

The vine gave its poison to them, and they left to distribute it to their tribes. Now, once where the vine held poison, there are only flowers. The water became safe for the tribes.

THE MAIDEN OF THE BIG LAKE

One young Indian maiden lived with her tribe near the shores of what is known today as Lake Drummond. She had an incredible beauty, while her soul and personality were warm as the summer sun. Many young men envied whoever won her heart and hand.

One young brave swift as the wind and courageous fell for her. And soon, they were to marry.

But close to their wedding date, the maiden grew deathly ill, and the medicine man couldn't do anything to help her. She died at night, adding to the light of the Spirit of the Swamp. It broke the young brave's heart, but he didn't reveal it in the lines of his face, for it was forbidden for men of the tribe to show their sorrow. The tribe buried her in the swamp's soft peat soil.

His love never forgotten in his heart, she roamed the warrior's dreams at night. She spoke to him from the top of a cypress tree, asking him to join her across the lake. On awakening, it felt so real to him that he ran through the woods and reeds, ignored the bears he passed, and other animals, too. He ended up deep within the swamp.

It was night and exhausted; he lay down on the ground and fell asleep. Once again, the maiden returned to him in a dream. She stood on the shore at the other side of the lake, begging him to join her. A bright light shone in the night sky above her, pointing the way to her. When he awoke, he knew where to find her.

He fashioned himself a canoe from young saplings, bark from nearby trees, and vines. Next, he made a lamp of sorts, filling it with fireflies to light his way in the dark. After launching it into the water, he paddled to the spot where her apparition had been in his dream. Of course, he never returned, nor was his canoe found at any shore around the lake. Mysteriously, the night grew black as a raven's wing and the only light that shone came from the firefly lamp, and that too vanished.

When the night has a new moon and clouds cover the sky, the stories tell if you see a hint of light from a firefly lamp on the dark lake, it's only the brave and his love, united, seeking the western shore, but never finding their way home.

LEGEND OF THE WHITE DEER

An Indian maiden, Wa-Cheagles, was a chief's daughter in one of two warring tribes in the Tidewater area. She made friends with a doe that she called Cin-Co, which meant "guiding friend." Stories were told that Cin-Co brought deer into the swamp each autumn and always brought her current fawn to Wa-Cheagles; the doe could always be found at the edge of the forest near a pool of dark brown water. This was the only way for the squaw to meet with Cin-Co, as squaws were not allowed into the forest because the tribes believed this to be an evil omen.

One year, Cin-Co appeared alone, limping. She walked back into the forest, coming and going two to three times. Wa-Cheagles followed and the doe led her to her fawn, which had a hoof firmly planted on a barely living rattlesnake. Wa-Cheagles believed the reptile had bitten Cin-Co and was the reason for her limp. She understood the doe wanted her to care for her fawn since the doe was dying from the poison. While there, Wa-Cheagles heard a moan from nearby, and she discovered an Indian brave from the enemy tribe of her people lying on the ground. His leg was swollen from a rattlesnake bite. She knew if she helped the brave, she must pledge herself to him. Doing this meant they would be hunted down and killed by arrows that had tips laced with water moccasin venom.

Wa-Cheagles took off her beret and tied it around his leg. Gathering some snakeroot, she applied a poultice over the wound. After making sure he was settled, and before she left, she saw that Cin-Co had died, and the fawn had vanished. She hurried back to her tribe.

For three days, she sneaked away to tend to the brave. On the third day, her father had followed her and found her in an embrace with the young man. He picked up Cin-Co's carcass and carried it away, giving them enough time to escape.

Wa-Cheagles and her lover stopped at Lake Drummond to rest. Three warriors had caught up with them and confronted them, determined to erase the curse from their tribe.

As the warriors drew back their bows to send their arrows flying, a dark cloud blotted out the sun, and a loud rustling noise filled the air. Wild geese flew in and surrounded Wa-Cheagles and her lover. More appeared and settled on the lake, covering it until not one inch of the water could be seen. Terrified, the braves dropped their bows and arrows and bolted.

The geese around the two lovers flew away. A "swamp spirit" rose out of the lake and strolled over the backs of the remaining geese, approaching the two lovers. It told them that Cin-Co's spirit had saved them and that Wa-Cheagles must continue the doe's good work. The spirit magicked the maiden into a white deer, a small crimson spot like a drop of blood on her forehead. Her lover became a charmed hunter. The spirit told them they would roam the swamp's forest forever, side by side, protected from both animals and hunters by rattlesnakes.

To this day, there are hunters and others who say they have seen the white deer and the Indian brave at her side. Whenever a hunter pursues the deer, a rattlesnake appears on the spot of the sighting, hissing and rattling its rattle.

OTHER HAUNTS, FOLKTALES AND LEGENDS OF THE GREAT DISMAL SWAMP

The Great Dismal Swamp is now owned by the government, and no one is allowed there at night (except maybe one of the park rangers). In the old days, it was an area most did not like entering at night, anyway. It takes nerve—loads of it. You never go left or right, but straight to your destination. Do not lose sight of your guide, or you may never see him again. In the daytime, there is a sameness about it. One wrong turn and you are lost. Without experienced help, you might end up in swampy mire or drown in the lake. But where daylight in the swamp can fill you with trepidation, when it is night and darkness surrounds you, it triples the dread. Even a full moon has trouble piercing the canopy of the trees.

White, glowing lights deep in the woods are common, will-o'-the-wisps willing to lead you until you are genuinely lost. Apparitions appear on the lake fishing or floating upright across the water. Phantoms of Indians still inhabit the swamp. Englishmen have lost their lives, and their spirits are seen wandering there. William Byrd may be seen hanging from a tall Tupelo tree. Whatever you do, don't try to assist him. He may exchange places with you, as no doubt, to be freed. Or vanish as soon as you come close enough.

The swamp water appears to be the color of tea, and there are those who claim it tastes like sassafras tea. Maybe not like clear mountain water, but that it is still drinkable. The Tantric acid that gives the water its color prevents it from stagnating.

Those who lived in the swamp claim that water from Lake Drummond is like a magic elixir and if you drink it, you will be free from malaria and other disorders, and you might even live for a hundred years.

There are tales that Blackbeard himself procured water for his irate crew from here and that Commodore Perry carried the swamp water on his voyage to Japan.

BURIED TREASURE

Sometime in the seventeenth century (I couldn't find anywhere about this vessel or even its name), a French ship had been blown off course as the crew fled a British warship. They found safety in the Chesapeake Bay and sailed up the Elizabeth River, where the ship ran aground near Dismal Swamp. Hearts beating in fear, the crew gathered as much of their plundered Dutch and Spanish gold coins as they could manage and abandoned ship, making their way into the woods.

The captain and his crew members found a spot and dug up earth, depositing the stolen loot deep into the ground and then covering it. Not long afterward, maybe as they bolted from the swamp inland or back to their ship (there's no mention of what they did after burying their ill-gotten gains), all were caught by British seamen and slain.

The story goes that, since then, people say they hear voices speaking in French, in the same area where, supposedly, the sailors had hidden their gold. The stories tell that the murdered phantoms of the French crew are still trying to guard the treasure.

SPIRIT DOG

An old widower, Old Man Wallace, lived with his daughter, Jenny, and an old hound dog he called Ham Bone, alone at the edge of the swamp. The dog had half its right ear gone, due to a fight with a mother raccoon protecting her babies.

Wallace made a living selling carvings made of swamp wood. Jenny did the cooking, cleaning, and gathering roots and berries from the swamp. Old Ham Bone always went with her.

One day, Jenny did not return. It was getting late, and her father was worried. Suddenly, Jenny came running up to their place, crying. She told him that she'd gotten lost, but that Ham Bone had guided her in the right direction. But when they came close to the swamp edge, a hole had opened up under Old Ham, and the hound fell into a pit hollowed out by a fire in the peat floor. He didn't look hurt, but Jenny couldn't reach him to get him out.

Both Wallace and Jenny went searching for the area, with Jenny leading him. They soon heard the dog howling and went in the direction of the sound, but as they approached the spot where they believed the sound was emanating from, they heard the dog howling from another direction. Jenny and her father searched all night, but they never found the dog. The howling had stopped, too. They continued the search during the daytime, but they could never locate the pit. The dog never returned home, and they gave up, the hound forgotten as they assumed, he had died.

Eventually, Wallace passed away, and Jenny left the swamp to live in the city.

Years passed, and now tourists and visitors frequent the swamp. One family visiting from out of state brought a canoe up the feeder ditch and stopped at a spot to have a picnic. After lunch, the parents relaxed while the daughter played. When it had grown quiet, the parents realized their daughter was nowhere in sight. Her father and mother called for her but didn't get a reply. Frantic, they were about to look for her in the swamp when the girl burst from between underbrush.

"Mama, Daddy, I had gotten lost in the swamp," she said, breathing hard. "I was scared, but this dog showed me the way back."

Both adults looked at where she pointed and saw an old motley hound with half its right ear missing. It turned and melted back into the bush. As they packed up to paddle their canoe back to where their vehicle was parked, they heard a hound howling somewhere in the distance.

THE BRIDE OF DISMAL SWAMP

A beautiful woman lived in Dismal Town at the edge of Dismal Swamp, and she was to marry a lumberjack. Her fiancée set out that morning to bag a deer for their wedding reception feast, but he never returned. Knowing he did not leave her at the altar and was maybe somewhere hurt, and still dressed in her wedding finery, she joined a search for him. She, too, never came back. Years passed, and hunters talked about seeing two apparitions in the early morning on the south side of the lake. One was a woman in her bridal gown sitting on a log and was baiting a hook, with a man beside her. Then, like smoke drifting away, both vanish. The legend says the couple found each other in the swamp, but they could not find their way back to Dismal Town.

THE PHANTOM LOVERS OF THE DISMAL SWAMP

A beautiful young woman fell ill only a few short weeks before her marriage. With his heart in pieces, her betrothed held her in his arms and watched as she gasped her last breath.

Inconsolable long after her body lay buried in the Dismal Swamp, he grieved for her day after day and night after night. Not eating the food his family gave him and not sleeping, he went mad with the obsession that she still lived. He figured her family had sent her away into the swamp, that she waited until he could come and rescue her. "I'll find her," he told his family, shaken by how he was acting. "I'll find her and hide her away from Death, so that fiend will never find her."

His family tried to talk him out of his mad scheme, but he didn't listen. He sneaked out that night and plunged into the swamp. He wandered for days, finally eating, though berries and roots, and he slept at night under trees in the marshland.

The young man stumbled upon Drummond's Pond one evening. A firefly blinked on and off as it skittered over the black surface.

He jumped up and down, excited. "It's my beloved! I see her light!"

Finding cypress branches, he constructed a raft and used it to float out to join his lost love. As his raft drifted close to the center of the pond, a wild wind arose, causing the waves to flip it, tossing the man into the waves where he sank beneath the murky water to drown

There are stories told that if one reaches Drummond's Pond after the last light fades and the fireflies come out, the phantoms of the man and his true love are seen floating on the raft. They are holding each other, and there is a firefly lantern in front of them. As the raft drifts away, it and the lovers dissipate, until only the light remains as a shining orb in the darkness.

THE WHITE DEER AND THE LIGHT

Black Jack was a hermit who took off in his boat one Christmas Eve, his only companion being his faithful hunting dog. He rowed across Drummond Lake, headed down Washington Ditch and landed near White Marsh Road. Both man and dog left the boat to hunt deer for their dinner.

The Native Americans in the area claimed that spirits protected the white deer. Jack's dog flushed out a white buck; the biggest deer Jack had ever seen. The buck froze, and when he fired at it, the bullet pierced its chest. But instead of falling, it bounded away. The dog gave chase, but could not keep up and eventually lost the trail. Jack began to wonder if the local Indian stories he'd heard were true.

Later, the dog found a red buck, and this one dropped when Jack's bullet hit it. He loaded the carcass in his boat and rowed for home. When it was almost dark, a blue-green light rose in the sky above the treetops. Jack thought it was the moon rising, but then it zipped for his boat. It paused above his boat and illuminated the whole lake. Frightened, the hermit began to row faster.

When he got to his cabin, he dropped the buck and gave an order to his dog to guard the carcass, then went inside to gather the items needed to clean and dress it. He changed his clothes, sharpened his knives, and went outside. Both his dog and the deer had vanished. Grabbing a lantern, he searched and found small patches of blood in the snow trailing back to the lake's edge. Stunned, he stood there, not knowing what to do.

Just then, a moan rent the air. Louder and louder, sounding as if it came from the middle of the lake. Black Jack stared as the same blue-green light rose out of the water and over a giant cypress, covering the tree in its unnatural glow.

When the scream of a wildcat filled the air, he jumped in his boat and raced downstream to the locks. He leaped onto the shore and bolted to Captain Crockett's cottage. It was midnight when he banged on the front door. Black Jack streaked past Crockett when he opened the door. For three hours, he sat in the cottage, not speaking, due to both feeling frozen and the shaking fear. Crockett gave him a mixture of honey, swamp water, and moonshine, and it freed him enough to blurt out his strange story.

The next morning Jack left, determined to find his dog and the missing deer. That night, Crockett dreamed of a white buck. A mysterious halo of light surrounded its head. He awoke, knowing it to be a premonition of danger for Black Jack. So, the next morning, he traveled to the hermit's cabin and found the door wide open and the fire out. Jack was not inside. He searched outside and found Jack in a kneeling position in a thicket. The hermit was frozen to death. No other tracks surrounded him, and Crockett saw no signs of a struggle.

Ever since then, on Christmas Eve between midnight and two in the morning, Black Jack can be heard gibbering about the light and the deer. At the break of dawn, his dog and the missing red buck have been seen where he died. And whenever hunters fire at a white buck, they never hit it. The deer and the dog vanish into the underbrush.

The white deer that hunters cannot shoot could be the Indian maiden, Wa-Cheagles from the Indian myths chapter, although they claim that it is a buck they saw and Wa-Cheagles became a white doe, protected by her warrior lover.

FAIRIES IN THE DISMAL SWAMP

A small island exists in the middle of the lake of the Great Dismal Swamp, an island that doesn't stay in one spot but moves to different places. It began as a log from which peat, trees, vines, and moss sprang to become a habitat, not for animals or birds of the swamp, but for something else. Swamp fairies who appear as flickering luminous orbs of light at night live on this island. The magical beings watch over all residing in the swamp, able to help when the need arises. Often referred to as mischievous gremlins, they protect the region. Although generally harmless, do wrong to one, and the wrath of the swamp spirits will locate you and lead you on a never- ending chase through the area, never to find your way out!

What Was It?

A man saw a ripple in the lake and watched as it rose a bit out of the water, emerging as a glowing object. Not from any emitted light, but the metallic reflection of the setting sun behind him. As it drew closer, he saw it not having any particular shape but a fluid like body undulating through the liquid and leaving a wake too small for its size and speed. The man watched it for about twenty minutes before it went back down into the depths of the lake.

He returned to the very spot many times, but never saw the entity again. Was it a trick played upon his eyes, or had he seen something unexplainable in Dismal Swamp?

WITCHES OF THE DISMAL SWAMP

Witch lore is varied in the Great Dismal Swamp, adapted to both the swamp and highland situations. Many of the stories concerning witches in the swamp have them leading hunters and their dogs astray for the sake of mischief. Some men claim they have wounded a witch with a silver shot, but again, there is no verification on these claims. One witch is said to have taken the form of a creepy stump beside Lake Drummond, all because she couldn't change herself back. Swampers tell that witches can take the form of a jack-o-lantern or will- o'-the-wisp and lure lost strangers with the illusion of a cabin's light waiting for them ahead.

Along the southwestern border of the swamp, they say a witch took the form of a jack-o-lantern and shot fire arrows at the occasional night traveler. In one area, a witch took the form of a deer to gather beans and corns from her neighbors nearby, hoping they would never discover it had been her.

Mostly, witches sought the swamp on nights empty of the moon and stars, so they could hear their own shrieking echoes and be with restless wraiths that haunt there. They would conjure up spirits and weave spells upon the unsuspecting inhabitants of the local communities. The stories go that the screams of these witches can be heard off the pathways on a dark moon or a drizzly night.

WITCH TALES

Many tales of witches spring from the swamp, from cannibal witches to hermit witches to the tale of an innocent woman accused, maligned, and killed for being a witch. The latter now haunts the Pasquotank River.

There is a legend told about a witch in the swamp that can change herself into a white-tailed doe upon seeing a hunting party, leading their dogs through the swamp until nearly dying from exhaustion. Though, that story doesn't scare hunters away.

An old hunter entered the swamp with a Native American guide leading the way. They walked upon the witch in human form. Startled, she changed into a white-tailed deer and darted away.

The hunter's dogs gave chase. This time, the witch's wiles failed her. The skillful native guide had the dogs chase her into a bog filled with briars and brambles. Caught by the thorns and vines on one side and the dogs on the other, the witch turned herself into a tree stump rather than be caught. The stump looked like a deer frozen in mid-leap.

The guide called on an acquaintance who happened to be the Devil. The dark angel showed up with the snap of two fingers (This makes me suspect the witch wasn't the only one in the area). Meanwhile, the hunter stood quiet and waited.

The Devil brought with him a powder made of dried bear liver, dried toads, and ground-up rattlesnake rattles.

Both he and the guide sprinkled the concoction around the base of the stump, and suddenly, a huge flame surrounded it.

The Indian guide danced and chanted. Lightning flashed, and thunder rumbled. "Now, the old witch will never roam the swamp again," he told the hunter.

Which she never did. Some insist that the witch is still leading hunting canines awry, causing them to disappear forever. Maybe even shifting into tree form and luring the dogs into the water to drown.

THE BLOOD WITCH

Great Uncle Breton always told about the time he had an encounter with a bloodsucking witch in the Great Dismal Swamp when he was only ten. The sun had set, and a fog rolled in, darkening the whole area, and he felt he had gotten lost. Hoping he might still be able to find his way out before complete darkness of night, he ran. A woman dressed all in red appeared beside him, reaching out to touch his arm, introducing herself as Pearl, and reassuring him she wouldn't harm him. Pearl invited him to come home with her until at least the rising moon cleared the fog.

She escorted Breton to her small cabin, where she provided a warm meal and a comfortable chair in which he fell asleep. He awoke to find her kissing him on his forehead. Not sure how long he'd been sleeping and wanting to be left alone, he withdrew from her. But she said she wanted only to give him another kiss and then she would leave him alone. Then she pulled him to her and placed her lips on his, and he fell back to sleep, this time much deeper.

When Breton awoke again, he found himself lying in the grass in the woods. The sun shined right into his eyes, and he heard birds singing. He tried to get up but felt weakened. Worse, neither Pearl nor her cabin were anywhere to be seen. Breton inched his way along until he came to a nearby creek for a long drink of water to hopefully restore himself enough to make his way home. When he looked up, he understood where he was, and Breton dragged himself until he made it back home just before the sun vanished behind the tree line. Once home, he discovered he'd been gone for three days. His mother bent over to hug him, but she screamed and backed away, staring at his throat. Teeth marks marred the flesh there.

WHAT HAPPENED TO RONNIE KAT?

Ronnie Kat spent some time at a local tavern with friends one night late in the nineteenth century, drinking until midnight. They left the establishment and stumbled their way along a path that cut through the dangerous Dismal Swamp.

A bright light appeared. One of Ronnie's friends who hadn't drunk as much as the rest, said, "Looks like a jack- o-lantern floating in the mire."

Curious about it, the drunken Ronnie took off, exclaiming, "I'm going to catch that thing!"

Suddenly the light morphed into a fiery arrow and flew at Ronnie. A bright flash blinded his companions, and the crackle of a lightning strike filled the air, and they all fell to the ground, trembling in fear. When they finally looked up, they only saw a large yellow cloud of smoke where Ronnie had been.

The next morning, men from the village nearby returned to the spot of Ronnie's disappearance. The only thing they found was a set of footprints in the mud, stopping mid-step as if something had snatched him away.

WITCH OF PASQUOTANK

There are tales about a witch who lived alone in a small cabin under some pine trees in the Great Dismal Swamp. Always cruel to those of Pasquotank, they feared her and believed she visited at night, changing the unlucky person into a horse that she rode all night until exhausted. The people thought that she'd become angry with them as a deadly plague hit their livestock. Several people also came down with this plague, and none of the local herb women could cure them, so they wasted away and perished.

Anger overcame their fear of the witch, and the community rushed to her cabin and seized her. And although she professed her innocence, they still marched her to the Pasquotank River, weighed her down with bricks, and tossed her into the water.

She drowned, which was proof of her innocence, but it was too late. There are claims that at the Old River Bridge, her apparition is seen, just below the waterline, floating down the dark water of the river.

This story is not real, as I learned that no witch had been hanged or drowned in Virginia, except the one the sailors hung from the ship when they came to Jamestown. Someone accused of witchcraft had been dunked in a river in Virginia Beach, but she escaped her ropes and swam around—this was Grace Sherwood. They placed her in jail instead.

CANNIBAL WITCH

A young man named Jack lived in Currituck at the edge of the swamp. He was warned to never venture into the swamp, or a bear may kill and eat him.

Yet, as a teenager with a healthy curiosity, he wanted to explore this place. So, one day he went into the swamp, hiking until he had to admit he was lost. He noticed dark clouds blanketing the sky above the treetops. It grew so dark he couldn't see an arm's length away. Frightened, Jack stumbled about as he tried to find his way out. Worse, he could hear the growls of bears, screams of wildcats, and owls hooting. Finally, a single ray of light penetrated the forest canopy, illuminating an opening ahead. Jack gave a sigh of relief and headed for it. Once he stepped through, he spied a small shack in a clearing, where a tiny, old woman sat in a rocking chair on the porch. She appeared to be eating a piece of pie on a plate. He walked over to the building.

The old woman greeted him. Jack said, "I'm lost."

The woman smiled and said, "Would you like to sit a spell and have a drink of goat's milk?"

"Thanks. I would like that."

She got him the glass of milk, and he drank it, growing sleepy after that. The old woman led him to a trundle bed inside, where he lay down and fell asleep.

While he slept, she set up a large cooking pot, and when it was ready, she killed and cut him into pieces, boiling him for her dinner.

The moral of this swampers' tale is about listening to your elders' warning about going into the Dismal Swamp, for they were right, something did eat Jack!

BEWITCHED DEER

A hunter spied a large doe in the swamp and shot at it. Although he never missed at the range he fired from, the deer pranced around, as if mocking him for failing to hit her. He tried again and again, all with the same results. Beginning to believe magic might have a hand in his attempts, he took a small piece of silver from his pocket and rammed it into the gun barrel. He fired one more time, and this time, the doe looked surprised and fell.

She managed to get to her hooves and took off through the dense underbrush. At the spot she'd fallen, the hunter saw a pool of blood and a blood trail leading into the swamp. He followed it, tracking his quarry through shallow pools and the tangle until he approached a cabin. A young boy was playing outside.

The hunter inquired as to the boy's family, and the lad told him that his great-grandmother had just died. She had suffered from a terrible pain in her side.

ANOTHER ENCHANTED DEER TALE

The story goes that one old lady referred to as Aunt Paula, lived in the area of the swamp, and hated "the deer hunters" who intruded on her land and scared her livestock and animals. She even broke off her wedding when she found out her husband-to-be had a love for hunting that far exceeded his love for her. After that, she would take off into the swamp for two to three weeks at a time.

Hunters blame her ghost whenever they shoot a deer but find no trace of its body where it had fallen, not even blood on the ground. They call it the "enchanted deer" and believe Paula is playing games with them.

WITCH SKIN

A young witch named Louise (Lou) Becker lived at the edge of the southwestern part of the Great Dismal Swamp. Lou and her husband lived in a two-room cabin, happy to be together. The husband didn't know about her magical abilities.

He would wake up at night and find her not in the cabin. He figured she was using the outdoor privy or stepped out for fresh air, but this kept happening a lot and for a long time. One night he pretended to sleep to see what his wife was doing during the nighttime.

When she slipped out of bed and stepped into the main room, he snuck out and crept after her. He was shocked as he watched his wife slip out of her nightgown and shed her skin, before she departed through the keyhole in the door. He knew only a witch could do this, so he understood this had to end. For all he knew, she might be wreaking havoc on their neighbors.

He went over to the kitchen side of the room, taking two canisters down from the cupboard. One tin contained salt, the other pepper. He placed the skin on the table and shook salt and pepper on the inside of it. Satisfied with his work, he returned the canisters to the cupboard, replaced the skin where it had lain, and crawled back into bed.

Not long before the sun would rise, Lou came back to the house and tried to slip her skin back on. Instead, she knew something was wrong with it and leaped away from it, frightened. Something was definitely wrong with her "skinny." She tried again, but the few more times she did, she couldn't get her skin back on.

The witch stomped back into the bedroom and sat on the bed in the raw. She understood what happened as she saw her husband snickering.

THE WITCH OF CORAPEAKE

A poor, aged woman lived alone in a cabin on the western border of the Great Dismal Swamp, not far from the village of Corapeake. She gathered roots, fruits, and berries to eat, but not enough to sustain her through winter. Too proud to beg, she nevertheless was grateful when some of her neighbors gave her gifts of food. Now, some believed her to be a witch, but no one ever accused her. Although they suspected, she took the form of a white doe and grazed on the peas, corn, and beans of their fields.

She felt no one suspected, but the villagers knew. They never bothered the white deer when it fed during the twilight.

WITCHY LOVE

At the beginning of the 20th Century, an old widower who'd lost his wife a few years before he courted a middle-aged woman. He found himself wanting to see her more and more, coming by her place most nights. When he fought to stay home at night, he would have visions of rats and cats running through his house and over his feet, while bats flew around the rafters. He told others about this.

They said, "A witch is pestering you."

They told him to get a silver knife, so he could use it to contact the witch that was causing the problems. He did just that, not finding any silver knives in the village, but from a chest full of excellent utensils his grandfather had left him, which included a sharp, silver carving knife. The next night, he waited as he ate his supper, the knife beside his plate.

When a strange cat slipped inside through a hole by his door and jumped upon his table, he thrust the knife at it, severing one of its toes. The feline ran away, yowling in pain. The next morning instead of a cat toe, he found a woman's finger. On the finger was the gold ring he had presented to his lady friend a few nights ago.

When he visited her, he found her with a cloth bandage around her hand, and he knew it had been her. Her spell over him ended, and he stayed away from her after that. Realizing he knew, and that meant the others knew, the witch moved away.

DEMONS AND HELL'S FIRE

HELL'S FIRE

There are tales to explain why people and animals disappear in the swamp. They persist of a place from which there is no return and not on any map, and that only those with evil in their hearts will find this portal to Hell itself. This supernatural doorway is covered by the numerous long ferns, so that no one will come upon it. Only those who have done wrong or harm to others, or the world in general, can discover it and enter the "Ring of Hell. They sink slowly into the soft, moist peat just like one would in quicksand. They cannot escape it, as Satan grabs hold of their legs and yanks them down into his world of eternal damnation.

There are those logical beings who believe that a cavern of burning peat lies beneath the surface, ignited by a lightning strike many decades before.

Whether a cavern of burning peat or due to the Devil, the result for those caught in this spot is an eternity in "Hell's Fire."

WOOD DEMONS' LIGHT

The legend says that if you stand on the shores of Lake Drummond at midnight and see a beam of light coming down from the star-filled night above, that is the light of the wood demons. It always concentrates on one area of the lake. The Swamp Fairies call upon the Great Spirit of the Swamp to bring down this light to soothe the wood demons that dwell in the forest and bathe in the lake at night. For when the demons are angry, they cause storm clouds to fill the sky and prevent the light from reaching the fairies' small island.

The Wood Demons in their fury, cause giant waves to churn the waters over the log island and sending the fairies to hide on the mainland. The Wood Demons will spread the fires to start in the woods, open beaver dams, and fell trees upon paths the animals use.

TALES OF SLAVES IN THE GREAT DISMAL SWAMP

THE RUNAWAY SLAVE

They say between 1853 and 1854 many slaves ran away and hid in the Great Dismal Swamp. They remained quiet during the daytime, but at night, they conducted their business by moonlight.

One man had gone into the swamp when a giant African figure appeared. This person wore no clothing except for a pair of torn britches and a tattered blanket over his broad shoulders, carrying a flintlock long rifle. He had his head bare of hair except a raggedy beard flecked with gray.

Years of hard living, along with fear and ferocity, were etched into the lines of his face. Each movement he made betrayed a life of caution and staying alert. He lifted his gun and pointed, and with a nod, he directed the way home for the lost stranger. The young man followed that way and tracked his way out of the darkness. As for the other, when he looked back, he saw no one. Had he met a specter of a slave who had gotten lost himself, swallowed by the darkness of the swamp, and spent his afterlife helping others lost in the dark swamp?

THE INSURRECTION OF NAT TURNER

Nat Turner was a slave born on a plantation in Southampton County in Virginia, October 2, 1800.

Other slaves believed he would be a prophet, and he thought he received messages from God. Spending many hours in the woods and swamp, he communed with spirits who told him he was meant for a great purpose in life. To him, blood on the corn determined that Jesus Christ would return to the earth. When he saw lights in the sky, he prayed for the meaning behind them. He preached the *Bible* among the slaves, and when a solar eclipse and unusual atmospheric event happened, it inspired his insurrection. Originally scheduled for July 4th, Nat became ill, so it began on August 21, 1831. That evening Nat met with five other slaves to plan the annihilation of the white population. They started at the home of Joseph Travis, killing five people in their beds with hatchets and knives, before they continued, amassing more slaves, guns, and ammunition while murdering the plantation owners. They passed by many poor whites, an indication that this uprising was not racial. As a militia was sent to capture and execute those involved, Nat Turner eluded capture by escaping into the Great Dismal

Swamp, where he lived off the land. Eventually, a hunter while out deer hunting came across his camp and took Nat captive. Nat Turner surrendered peacefully and was brought to trial in Southampton County in November 1831. They tied him up, tortured him, whipped, and hung him along with 16 of his recruits. They delivered Nat's body to doctors, who skinned and made grease from his body.

To this day, tales are told of his spirit seen running through the canebrakes in the swamp, skinless and alone.

THE OLD MAN OF THE SWAMP

An ex-slave appeared in Chesapeake near the Dismal Swamp after the end of the War Between the States. He had returned home after many years to confess to a crime he'd made many years ago. The old man was shocked as he didn't recognize the town, nor did he find a single soul who remembered him.

He had fled from his mater's farm to the swamp after killing a white man in a dispute over a fish entangled in both his and the other man's lines. When the white man tried to yank the fish away, exclaiming it belonged to him, the young slave grabbed the other's hatchet and buried it in the man's forehead.

Frightened, he weighed the man down and then pushed him into the water. He ran away before anyone discovered what he had done.

Some older people dimly remembered the incident, but they dismissed it, claiming it was so long ago that they weren't sure of the details. If it had been a murder, they assumed the perpetrator had been caught. As for the local constabulary, he wasn't too interested in something he thought the old man had made up.

But the old man felt determined to confess and pay for his crime.

"Please," he said, "the white man's haint is haunting me, won't leave me alone, but wanting revenge. I can't take it anymore. It follows me everywhere."

Some claimed that they saw him walking the dusty road back to the swamp, where he faded away before their eyes.

And just like his victim's spirit, his punishment seemed to be that he couldn't convince any of the living of his crime and was destined to face the other for all eternity.

TALL TALES

SNAKES

One man from Suffolk was out hunting in the swamp when he saw snakes moving along the ground from all directions. He followed them and came upon what appeared to be a lump of snakes big as a barrel. He fired at them, and many snakes disbanded, fleeing, but when he came near, he saw what he thought to be a hundred lying dead and many more wounded. The man found a ten-foot rod and measured one of the snakes, finding it to about twenty feet long!

He told his friends about it the next day, but many thought he was spinning them a tall tale, as no one has ever seen a snake the length of his description.

FOUNTAIN OF YOUTH

It's believed that the swamp enables people to live longer lives. Swampers claim that the brown tantric water of the swamp cured what ailed them, from rheumatism to the retardation of aging. They even believed that animals drinking this water grew bigger and turned into monsters. The local Indian tribes told of a pool deep in the swamp, hidden from humanity, that held magical healing properties. The beasts and fowl of the swamp knew where this was and journeyed to it whenever they were ill or injured.

Wine made from berries grown in the swamp is considered magical, the spirits having grown in the waters of the healing Dismal Swamp. Of course, drink enough, and one can be anything.

THE TRAPPED SCHOONER

Long ago, when the area flooded, a schooner from the ocean found its way into the swamp. Trapped there, the men either drowned or fled to die in the swamp elsewhere. It remained there for years, and people told of visiting it. Supposedly, when they built the canal, the rotting timbers were dismantled and taken away. But to this day, when a storm rises from the southern horizon, people claim to see a two-masted schooner sailing north along the Great Dismal Swamp canal.

THE DEER BELONGED TO JULIUS CAESAR

One man called Johnny Culpepper used to tell visitors tall tales. He was always known as being "Full of It," that is, stories of Dismal Swamp.

Besides telling these, he also was famous for double talk, or as he called it, "bear Latin."

One of those stories he told concerned the time he was out hunting and came across a buck so big that he couldn't count the number of points on the animal's antlers. He shot it, and when he walked over to it he found a strap around its neck with a tag attached, with words etched on it. "When Julius Caesar here did reign, About my neck he hung this chain; And whoever shall take me, Save me for Julius Caesar's sake."

GIANT MOSQUITOES

Swampers would tell tales about the giant-sized mosquitoes inhabiting the swamp that could carry away an unsuspecting adventurer. One drunken Swamper full of shine claimed that two of those monsters ate one of his prize cows- hooves, bone, and all. After that, they perched upon an old cypress tree and rang the cow's bell, trying to lure the cow's calf to them. When it came galloping up, they took to flight and seized it. Both argued about where they would take it. One wanted to carry it to the swamp, but another disagreed, worried that the even bigger mosquitoes might take it from them.

PARANORMAL ACTIVITY IN THE GREAT DISMAL SWAMP

One park employee was driving his truck along Washington Ditch with his dog in the passenger seat, when his headlights lit up and revealed a man and woman in Colonial garb walking side-by-side. He stopped his vehicle and got out, going to ask if they needed any help. His dog was in a frenzy barking at the couple. The employee turned to shush the animal, but when he turned back to the couple, both were gone. He searched around his truck and even went a bit into the woods but didn't see them.

As he drove away, it hit him that maybe he saw something supernatural. Fear crept over him. Another park employee he told the story to years later, thought it might be the bride and groom from the second story told in this chapter, who went into the swamp and never returned. Their ghosts are said to haunt the Washington Ditch Trail at night, always walking toward Dismal Town, but never making it home.

SASQUATCH/SKUNK APE IN THE GREAT DISMAL SWAMP

There have been "Skunk Ape" sightings from the swamps of Louisiana and Georgia to the Great Dismal Swamp. The Dismal Swamp has a haunting beauty. It is a geological wonder, and all kinds of reptiles, large and small mammals, birds, flowers, giant trees, and beautiful ferns inhabit it. One can believe that the Skunk Ape might also exist there.

In October of 1982, a young man named John was hunting in his deer stand when he saw a massive creature come into view from the waist up. Even though it was about fifty yards from his tree, he could smell its horrible odor wafting up to him. Either it didn't know he was there, or it didn't care, for it stood there, eating leaves. Many would say he saw a bear standing up on its hind feet, but with such a good, long look at it, he knew it wasn't any animal that was known to exist in the swamp. It had hands like a human, black, with hair on the back of them. The face looked mainly hairy, except around the eyes. The neck was short and stubby, with a kind of furry ridge that ran up the back of its neck, to the top of what appeared to be a slightly pointed head that sloped down to a gorilla-like forehead.

After a while, it walked away, though he continued to hear the crunch of sticks and leaves for five minutes before that too ended. It scared him, but he managed to get down from the stand and head back to find his hunting companions.

In 2000, a camp counselor left twelve sleeping campers with her co-counselor and went to take a shower. At 11p.m., everyone was either asleep or inside their cabins, preparing to go to sleep. Suddenly, noise erupted from the wooded area west of the bunkhouse. At first, she wondered if it was some of the others playing around. But the sound seemed to be coming from one individual— it was a loud howl that morphed into a whining bark that ended almost like a hoot. It puzzled her because, although knowledgeable in the sounds of wildlife, she had never heard anything like it. A human couldn't make the sound, yet it seemed eerily human-like.

The young woman left the circle of light that came from the shower building and headed back to the cabins. Her cabin happened to be the last one, and there were no porch lights on. None of this bothered her until the noise filled the air again. Much closer and much louder too, it frightened her. She walked faster. The howl repeated itself, sounding as if whatever it was had drawn closer, parallel to her path. The young woman broke into a run, and after reaching her cabin, entered it and locked the door behind her. She didn't hear anything else after she got inside, but of course, that may be because she put on her Discman to calm herself down and drown anything else out.

Another sighting concerned a man and his wife. They had been walking the Great Dismal Trail for one mile when they sat down at one of the benches along the path. As they did so, they heard what sounded like someone walking parallel to the canal on the other side, like leaves being crunched underfoot and twigs snapping, as if by a two- legged man. Five minutes later, the sounds ended in front of them. Then they started hearing steps coming from the left side, and a couple of minutes later, chattering erupted from both the center point and to their left. Freaked out, the man used a small, thick pine branch and hit it against a mile marker post a couple of times to see what would happen. Ten to fifteen seconds later, the man and his wife heard a similar banging coming from the area of the footsteps, except deeper into the woods.

The canal is about forty or fifty feet across and very deep; the brush on the other side is dense like a thick wall. Unable to see what made the sounds, the man thought it might be best if he and his wife left. But his wife wanted to see what it was, so they headed back the way they had come. They found a park ranger in his vehicle waiting to close the gates. As he knew of frequent black bear sightings in this area, the husband inquired how bears might make sounds in the wild. He described the chattering and asked if the bears could do that. The ranger said he didn't think bears produced that sort of sound. They talked a little more, then his wife and he left the ranger and headed for their vehicle. But when they were only twenty feet away from the car, they heard a loud but short yell from the direction of the swamp. It sounded like a cross between a whoop and a woman's scream.

THE AUTHOR'S EXPERIENCES IN THE SWAMP

Bill and I headed for Suffolk back in November 2016. We would do the ghost tour that night, but this made it an excellent opportunity to check out Dismal Swamp that morning. We thought to drive to the lake, except there had been a fire. The fires no longer threatened the woods, but they smoldered beneath the lake for months afterward, and the park wouldn't allow anyone to drive to the lake. Instead, I walked the wooden trail, snapping pictures along the way, and using my recorder. Nothing supernatural happened to me that day, nor did anything out of place appear in my photos or on the audio.

The first time my husband and I returned to the swamp was on April 30th, 2019. It was sunny, and after stopping by the U.S. Fish and Wildlife Refuge Center, we drove to enter the park at the nearest entrance. Along the way, I made Bill stop so I could get out and snap some pictures. After I was back home and had uploaded the photos, I found one with this weird anomaly circling a tree stump. A friend who investigates with me for

Paranormal World Seekers, Carol Smith, looked at it carefully and said it looked like energy.

Underground Railroad Pavilion boardwalk at Dismal Swamp

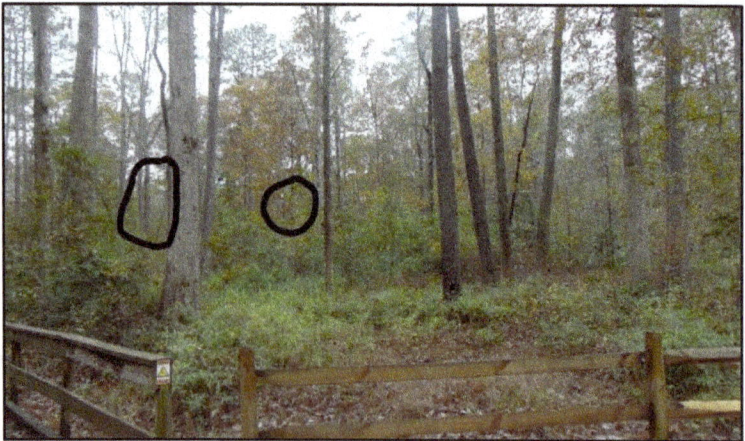

In the photo above, I circled possible faces, form. One had a skull face, something else standing there on the opposite side of the picture. Both were not in another photo of the same area. This was taken November 17, 2019, the first road we went down.

Here is a close-up version of the photo.

We saw birds and turtles along the way, especially when the land became fields with only trees in the distance. Eventually, we came to Lake Drummond, where many legends concerning it have been told for years. It looked odd to see trees sprouting out of the water. But it also had a wondrous beauty about it. It didn't seem spooky to me. We left after a while, heading for home.

AUTHOR'S VISIT AND INVESTIGATION NOVEMBER 17, 2019

We returned on Sunday, November 17, 2019. It must have rained the night before as everything looked wet, and it was colder than the previous day, although the wind was not as bad. Many trees had taken on the costume of autumn, with various colors, and the gray, cloudy skies gave an aura of spookiness not there back in April. This time, the center was closed, so we couldn't stop there. We drove down the same road we had taken back in April, but we stopped at the sign that required us to purchase a permit to be allowed to drive our car down to Lake Drummond.

Of course, not having enough change and no checks, I ended up doing a ghost box and EVP session there before taking some pictures.

I turned both the recorder and the ghost box on, setting the latter to scanning radio stations.

"Are there any spirits here in Dismal Swamp?"

"Who is connected to the Underground Railroad I see happened here? Anyone who became part of the maroon colony here?"

"Is the bride and her husband who'd been seen by a park ranger still haunting here? Any Colonial spirits here?"

"Philip," a male voice uttered from my ghost box. A woman also replied, "Colton."

"First name?"

She said, "Fran."

Again, the male said, "Philip."

"How many spirits are here right now?"

A male voice said, "10." But not actually hearing that at the time and thinking I heard nine, I asked if it was nine, and the same spirit said, "No!" (I heard all this better in the quiet of my home, off the laptop, and with headphones).

"Any ghost here connected to that slave rebellion that happened around here, where many white people were killed?"

A male voice uttered, "Bleed."

"Are any natives here, of local tribes?"

I didn't get any answer to that, but again, this might be due to them not understanding English.

I attempted something else. "Have you seen pirates around here back when you were alive? Like Blackbeard?"

Nothing.

"Any ghosts here?"

A male voice said, "Yes." Then, I got, "John. Philip." I said, "Dismal Swamp looks haunted to me."

What sounded like the same male voice replied, "It is." "Anybody died here and is buried in the swamp?"

I got, "Three."

I said, "Goodbye. I'm leaving now, so don't follow me home, please. Good day."

A man called out from the box. "Goodbye."

I did a quick EVP session after I shut off the box. I asked several questions, but only one got me an EVP. I inquired if anyone had drowned in Lake Drummond and I did get "Lake Drummond."

We drove to the Washington Ditch Canal and drove down the road to the parking lot. I grabbed the ghost box and recorder and slung my camera around my neck, leaving Bill in the car.

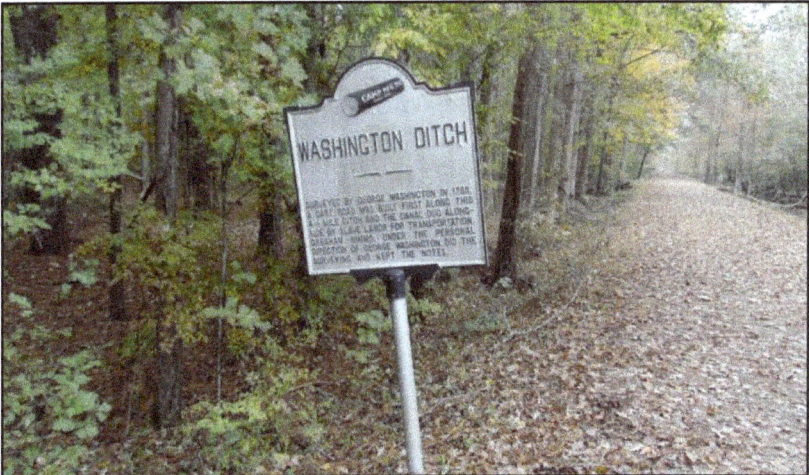

Sign saying this is the Washington Ditch and Canal. The word "dug" mentioned in it had come up when I had asked about slaves.

I read the signs I saw there, taking pictures of them. One mentioned Washington Ditch and said: "Surveyed by George Washington in 1763. A cart road was built along this 4 ½ mile ditch, and the canal dug alongside by slave labor for transportation. Gresham Nimmo, under the personal direction of George Washington, did the surveying and kept the notes."

The other was about Dismal Town. It said, "Washington and company used this spot as their Dismal Swamp headquarters. The town was built prior to the Nimmo Survey of 1763 on Riddick 402 Acre Patent."

Now there is a word here that would come up three times in my ghost box session. At the time, I heard it and thought of the family who had it as their last name whose house was in Suffolk, but after listening to the recordings and looking at the picture, it was clear what the ghosts were trying to say.

I turned on both the ghost box and recorder, and I began. "Any spirits here?"

Something answered but spoke too low. "Names?"

"Riddick."

"Washington and company? George Washington?" "Riddick." Second time for that word.

"Are there any spirits of slaves here? Connected to here or the swamp?"

A female voice from my box said, "Dug." (With slaves digging the canal, I understood later when I was home that this was a slave who dug the canal).

"Why are you still here?"

Something answered, but again too low. "Do you feel you're stuck to this land?" "Marked."

"Names?"

Once again, I got the word, "Riddick."

I said, "I am going now. Goodbye. Good day." A male voice from my box uttered, "Good day."

I switched off the ghost box and the recorder, before hurrying back to the car. We still had two places in downtown historic Suffolk to investigate, and it was already 3:00 p.m. I needed to get home to eat and get all the audio and pictures uploaded.

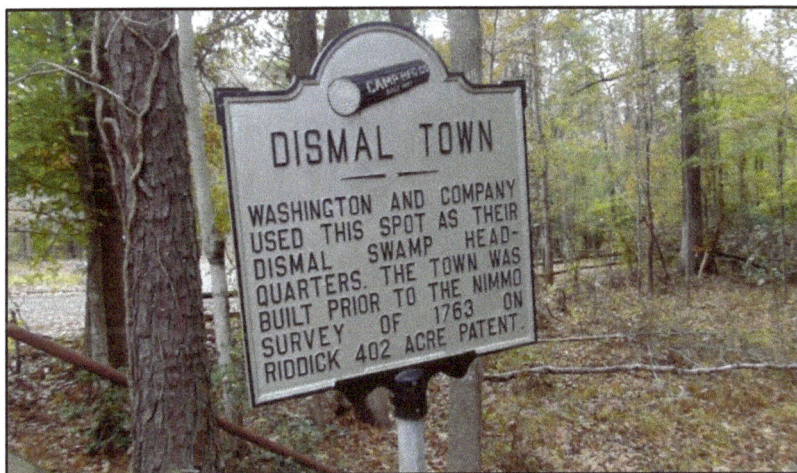

The word Riddick came over three times through my ghost box and it hit me what the spirits were telling me after looking at the sign in this photo.

Those who live in the area and tourists who visit claim they see wispy white things, especially around the lake, but no doubt what they saw could be foxfire, a substance given off when certain fungi decay wood. Again, maybe they did see something. The place can be eerie, especially if shrouded in fog or mist. And besides spirits, you might run into Bigfoot or fairies. Do take care and don't strike out alone in the woods and head off the designated trails, for you never know who or what you might meet. You might encounter more than animals and birds in the Great Dismal Swamp, and the haunts and Bigfoot are waiting to welcome you, even if it means taking the portal to Hell.

CRYPTID AND UFO ENCOUNTERS FROM SURRY TO SUFFOLK

"If incredible creatures like sharks can exist, why not Bigfoot? When I look at sharks, they're the most terrifying, monstrous, dinosaur-like things. To this day, I'm so fascinated by them and can't get my head around how they are on Planet Earth at all."
~Rachael Taylor

Besides ghosts and ghouls, Virginia also can boast it has monsters. The Commonwealth has had the oldest sightings of Sasquatch, going back before the English landed on its shore, with stories coming from the Virginia tribes of Native Americans. It seems there is not one area in the state that the hairy giant hasn't been encountered. That included the counties and cities along Routes 10 and 460 South. (I have Bigfoot stories in the Great Dismal Swamp chapter, so they won't be here. Except the one I found in my book, *Haunted Virginia: Legends, Myths, and True Tales*).

BIGFOOT ENCOUNTERS

CLEAR PHOTO OF BIGFOOT?

Not sure if this encounter happened around Suffolk, but it was reported to happen at a remote Creekside, about five miles from civilization off the intercoastal waterway. This could even be at Dismal Swamp or its canal in Chesapeake, right beside Suffolk. A *Cryptozoology News* article, along with being reported on Fox 2 News in 2014, has a man claiming he has the first non-blurry image of Bigfoot. They were taken by his dad and his father's friend "Uncle Jap," while fishing at the same location both men had supposedly spotted the cryptid 25 years ago. It happened around 9:00 p.m. After feeling something was watching them from some bushes, his father handed him a shotgun and told him to shoot where he felt it was. He did, and they heard bloodcurdling screams after the shot. It apparently bolted from the bushes and into the water. Of course, that scared them enough to be frightened all night and the next morning, they found a path that had been cleared by the creature as if "a skid steer had gone through the woods." YouTube users have argued it's just a tree stump. Is it, or not? You decide.

You can see the video at https://www.youtube.com/watch?v=PzkwOYR_jyE.

COUPLE ENCOUNTER BIGFOOT IN THE GREAT DISMAL SWAMP

In 2008, a man and his wife were following the Great Dismal Trail when they heard someone walking alongside the canal running parallel to the trail. The sound of the footsteps passed them and was soon ahead of their position, at which point they stopped. They heard chattering noises from the bushes up ahead so, thinking quickly, the man picked up a stick and rattled the bushes. The hikers heard the footsteps begin again, leading away from their position.

As the couple left the park, they discussed the encounter with the park ranger. The ranger commented the noises were not the type made by black bears living in the area and really didn't have an explanation. As the hikers returned to their car, they suddenly heard a short, loud scream from the swamp. It was unlike any noise they had ever heard before and the couple were keen amateur photographers who spent a lot of time in the outdoors.

Was it a Bigfoot they encountered, or something else?

BIGFOOT SIGHTED BY MAN AS A CHILD

A man named Ronnie in an article on a website called Bigfootly.com and at the Virginia Bigfoot Research Organization website, shared his story of encountering Bigfoot when he was a child growing up in Nansemond County.

He was 12 to 13-years old at the time of his incident, which occurred in the fall of 1974, and he lived in the little town of Driver. He mentioned about walking home from Driver Middle School instead of riding the bus. It was about a 2 to 2 ½ miles as he followed the railroad tracks, going through fields and woods to his neighborhood.

He figured it to be about late September or early October and he was walking down the tracks like he had done many times before when in the distance, maybe 50 yards away, he caught sight of a dark figure squatting down by the railroad tracks. The sound of a rock striking the tracks came to him, and Ronnie realized it came from the figure, so he stopped and watched for a minute. He realized it never noticed him. Suddenly, a small plane flew over, kind of low, and it must have startled whatever the being was, for it looked up. It rose from the crouch and in one stride, stepped over the tracks and easily stepped over the ditch on the other side of the tracks to head into the woods.

It appeared to be about seven feet tall, covered in reddish brown hair, and the creature's face seemed flat or maybe covered with hair because Ronnie couldn't remember any facial features.

This scared him enough that he backtracked about a half mile down the tracks and cut across a field to Nansemond Parkway, following the roads home instead of walking by where the creature had disappeared.

He never told anyone about it until about five years ago. He admitted to telling a select few people about his experience and discovered two others had seen creatures like he had – one in Windsor, and another in the Dismal Swamp.

BIGFOOT AT CHIPPOKES PLANTATION PARK

I found a story in a book about a Sasquatch incident that happened in the 1970s, on some beachfront near Chippokes Plantation Park. It concerned Ben Keyes from Prince George County, who is a paranormal investigator. He happens to own a cottage on private farmland on the beachfront.

One evening after waterskiing, Keyes went to find a missing slalom ski. He hoped it had washed ashore. It'd grown dusk, and as he made his way through the green foliage of a fallen oak tree, a foul odor wafted to his nose. It grew stronger as he walked. No doubt, he reasoned, it came from some dead animal. Suddenly, he saw a hulking shadow against the night sky. It moved and Keyes caught the odor he smelled earlier, more potent now.

Scared, he aimed his flashlight at what would be the shape's midriff. Realization came to him how tall this thing was. The creature stopped moving and Keyes saw its black fur shining in the light of his flashlight. In his estimation, he figured it to be at least eight or nine feet tall. He raised his light up to the head and saw dark eyes in what he thought to be a Cro-Magnon face. Thoughts flittered through his mind. Was it a bear or some escaped gorilla? He remembered that one should never make any eye contact with a wild animal and he shut off his flashlight, looking away. Fear made him also run into the river, even though he knew it was shallow for a few hundred feet and the thing could come after him. Chest deep, he stared back at the shore, but couldn't see the beast. At that moment, he heard the noise of an inbound motor. His sister and his friends had wondered what happened and worried, had been searching for him. He convinced them to go ashore with him to see if they could find the furry creature. In the light of their flashlights, they found massive footprints in the sand. By their size, they figured it had to weigh an awful lot. Sounds of some big thing crashing through the brush in the nearby wood and a nasty odor reached them. Frightened, they got back on the boat and headed back to the cottage.

Later, Keyes ran into two elderly brothers who lived and hunted in Surry all their lives. They told him about something taking muskrats out of their traps, and at one site, found footprints about eighteen inches long and wide. There was even a disgusting smell in the spot, as if whatever had been there had left not long before they came. One brother mentioned that one day as he set up a trap, he saw the creature. It looked like some giant, hairy humanoid standing upright on a hillside clearing, holding a muskrat in its grasp. Of course, until they told Ben Keyes their encounters, they never mentioned it to anyone else fearing that they would be ridiculed.

WEREWOLF SIGHTING

There were stories of a werewolf stalking the Dismal Swamp area on the Suffolk, Virginia side in the late 1800s to the early 1900s.

THREE TALES FROM THE GREAT DISMAL SWAMP

An eight-year-old boy who lived on the edge of the Great Dismal Swamp was in bed one night. The sky was cloudless, or just very bright (he never thought until recently as an adult whether the moon was shining or not) and saw a beast looking right through his window at him. He could see drool running from its fangs, and its eyes were looking straight at him. It was supposedly standing on its hind legs and had cream, red, and brown-colored, matted fur, and a face almost like a wolf's. Other than its snout, its facial features were very human, with high cheekbones; the area around its eyes and its eyes, too, appeared humanlike. He thought the eyes were yellow.

The boy crawled out of bed and ran straight to his mother's room, where she let him stay the night. In the morning, they looked around outside, and beneath his bedroom window they found grass yanked out, but no discernable footprints there or elsewhere in the yard. There were actual scratches in the wood under his window, and paint was missing.

Another encounter with beast was by Edward Smith. One night his dogs were making a racket and thinking that it might be a fox getting into his chickens, the man grabbed his shotgun and stepped outside. Suddenly, one of his dogs gave a loud screech. Worried that maybe it was something worse than a fox, he rushed into the yard. The moon lit the area, and he saw something standing over one of his hounds. Something way bigger than a fox.

It stood on its hind legs, much taller than his own six-foot height. He assumed it must be a bear, most likely rearing up onto its back legs. When the creature turned its head, the moonlight revealed not a bear's face, but what looked like a wolf's, with sharp, pointed ears, glowing yellow eyes, and a short snout that when it opened its maw, the moonlight glinted on sharp fangs. It stood easily on its hind feet as if that was natural to it.

Frightened, Smith shot at it twice. It whipped around and ran away on its hind legs like a man would, vanishing into the shadowy trees toward where the Dismal Swamp would be. Smith ran over to his dog and found it hurt, but not dead. The only blood he found came from his dog, but nothing to show him if he'd hit the creature.

Whatever the wolf thing was, he never had problems with it again.

Another encounter with the bipedal wolfman was by a little girl who was asleep in her bedroom when she heard sounds at the window. She looked up and saw a horrific face looking in at her. She screamed, and her parents rushed in seconds later. When she told her parents about her visitor, pointing at her window, they didn't see anything. She told them that it looked like a big dog or wolf. Her father grabbed his hunting gun and ran outdoors to search but found nothing.

The next morning, he did find large footprints in the dirt just under her window. The thing was, the window was about six feet from the ground and if a dog or wolf was looking in by rearing up on its hind legs, it had to be a very big animal. There were a few more incidents concerning the 'werewolf,' as people began calling it; hunters began hunting it. One man, Harrison Walker, claimed to have killed the monster, but he never showed a carcass, and sightings continued through to the early 1900s, until they finally stopped.

Was it a shapeshifter, a Dogman, or something else? We may never know.

UFO SIGHTINGS

"The Truth is Out There."
~X-Files TV Show

Yes, Virginia has ghosts, all due to its history, and even Sasquatch, since the oldest sightings came from here, too. But if you think beings from other worlds are visiting us, well, they are.

UFO OVER SURRY, VIRGINIA, APRIL 17, 2013

This was cited at latest-ufos.com. It was around 2053 hours on April 17, 2013 and a man was scanning the skies with a thermo-imaging camera when he noticed an object shaped like a boomerang coming from the west heading east. The boomerang slit off into four circles and became a tight formation. The witness grabbed his cell phone and began recording the screen while tracking the objects. He couldn't see the objects with the naked eye, but the thermo-imaging camera appeared to pick them up.

The photo can be seen here: https://www.latest-ufos.com/wp-content/uploads/2013/04/surry-ufo-sightings-virginia- 2013.jpeg.

Suffolk Sighting

The witness who reported this said she should have grabbed her camera. Her husband, a rocket scientist with NASA, had taken their dog out before bed. He came in and said that she needed to see what was in the sky, that it looked like a UFO. The woman grabbed her coat and slipped on her shoes so she could see what he was talking about. The couple remained outside about 10 to 15 minutes until the lights up in the sky began to fade. There were at least twenty, probably thirty of them. They moved slightly, but it was hard to tell, as they looked like very low stars blinking. Only they seemed to be green and red with blue, in contrast to most stars, which are white. They stayed low to the ground and it was only in one area, everywhere else there was nothing.

Second UFO Sighting in Suffolk in 2017

This happened at 5:27 p.m. on November 24, 2017, in Suffolk, right before sundown. The witness was on their cell phone when it happened. Five bright-colored orbs shot out from behind the top of the trees at a diagonal angle all in unison, slowing down after coming out from behind the tree line. Two of the orbs on the left merged into one orb at the same time as two orbs on the right. It had freaked the witness out as they thought it must be a commercial plane at first because of how big and close the lights were. Suddenly, the bright orbs became three and vanished as if they had never been there.

THIRD SIGHTING IN SUFFOLK

This report had me wondering where they lived in Suffolk, as there is that ghostly spook light seen on Jackson Road. The person looked out the bathroom window in March 2017 and saw a huge orange circle. It remained in the sky for a few minutes before it dropped to the ground. The person was adamant that it wasn't a shooting star, as it was too large and colored orange, almost like a fireball.

WAKEFIELD UFO ENCOUNTER

The witness for this UFO sighting was driving up 460 in August 2017, around Wakefield, when he saw this bright, light yellow/orange star hovering in the sky. It began to grow dim, when suddenly, it flashed bright as the sun, before dimming again after fifteen minutes. The person admitted to calling the local news to see if anybody else had reported the object.

Next time you're driving along Route 10 or 460 South, if you spot something standing alongside the road or hovering in the sky, just keep driving. Bigfoot most likely wants to be left alone and as for the flying object; it could just be interplanetary visitors on vacation.

CONCLUSION

"Death is no more than passing from one room into another."
~Helen Keller

   Reader, you have come to the end of your journey through the pages of this book. The next time you want to take a scenic drive in Virginia, maybe even head down to Virginia Beach and want to avoid the craziness of I-64, take Route 460 East, or even Route 10. Both will get you there. Just don't be surprised if you see a ghost or two. Maybe even Bigfoot, or a UFO flying overhead, or any other strange creature. More than peanuts, ham, and history are connected to this section of Southeastern Virginia. The paranormal has its claw hold there just like the rest of the state, and the dead are ready to SCARE you a good time.

Joseph Bridger's grave in the St Luke's Historic
Church in Smithfield.

Pamela K. Kinney gave up long ago trying not to ignore the voices in her head and has written horror, fantasy. science fiction, a children's fantasy picture book, poetry, nonfiction ghost books, and a nonfiction cryptid/indigenous mythology book, *Werewolves, Dogmen, and Other Shapeshifters Stalking North America*. Her horror short story, "Bottled Spirits," was runner-up for the 2013 WSFA Small Press Award and is considered one of the seven best genre short fiction for that year. Her poem, "Dementia," that was in the *HWA Poetry Showcase Vol VII*, got her a mention in Best Horror of the Years, Vol 13. Her faerie children's picture book, *Christmas Magic*, took second place in the Children's-Holidays category of the Book Fest Awards, Spring 2024. She has a story and a poem in *The Haunted Zone*, a charity horror anthology with stories and poetry written by women military veterans, a horror story published in the horror anthology, *Vinyl Cuts*, a story in *Halloweenthology: Witches' Brew*, and a poem included in the *Terror at Miskatonic Falls* anthology—all four anthologies were released in 2024. Her YA dark fantasy novel, first in the *Moon Ridge, Virginia* trilogy, *Demon Memories*, was released October 15, 2024. She is working on a new nonfiction ghost book for Schiffer Publishing, about ghosts/cryptids/UFOs on or near the Appalachian Trail, and the second book in the *Moon Ridge, Virginia* trilogy.

Pamela and her husband live with one crazy black cat (who thinks she should take precedence over her mistress's writing most days). Along with writing, Pamela has acted on stage and film and investigates the paranormal for episodes of *Paranormal World Seekers* for AVA Productions. She is a member of Horror Writers Association, Virginia Writers Club, and James River Writers. Learn more about her at https://PamelaKKinney.com.

BIBLIOGRAPHY

Clyne, Patricia Edwards. *Ghostly Animals of America.* New York, New York: Dodd, Mead, 1977.

Elton, P. M. *Ghostly Tales of Selected Stare Parks.* Cambridge, MN.: Adventure Publications, 2015.

Hauck, Dennis William. *Haunted Places, The National Directory.* New York, New York: Penguin Books, 2002. Kinney, Pamela K. *Haunted Virginia: Legends, Myths and True Tales.* Atglen, Pennsylvania: Schiffer Publishing, Ltd., 2009

Kinney, Pamela K. *Virginia's Haunted Historic Triangle 2nd Edition: Williamsburg, Yorktown, Jamestown, and Other Haunted Locations.* Atglen, Pennsylvania: Schiffer Publishing, Ltd., 2019.

Lee. Marguerite DuPont. *Virginia Ghosts.* Berryville, Virginia: Virginia Book Company, 1966.

Nesbitt, Mark, *Cursed in Virginia Stories of the Damned in the Old Dominion State.* Guilford, Connecticut: Globe Pequot, 2017.

Taylor, L. B. *Monsters of Virginia: Mysterious Creatures in the Old Dominion,* Mechanicsburg, Pennsylvania: Stackpole Books, 2012.

The Big Book of Virginia Ghost Stories. Mechanicsburg, PA.: Stackpole Books, 2010.

The Ghosts of Tidewater and Nearby Environs Williamsburg,

Virginia: self-published 1990.

The Ghosts of Virginia Volume I. Williamsburg,
      Virginia: self-published 1996

The Ghosts of Williamsburg Volume II. Williamsburg,
      Virginia: self-published Fourth Printing,
      2010.

Traylor, Waverly. *The Great Dismal Swamp in Myth
      and Legend,* Rosedog Books, First Edition,
      2010.

Tucker, George Holbert. *Virginia Supernatural Tales:
      Ghosts, Witches and Eerie Doings,* Donning
      Company Publishers, 1977.

CONTACT INFORMATION FOR THE SITES VISITED

Bacon's Castle's address is 465 Bacon's Castle Trail, Surry, Virginia 23883. For further details about its history, tours, admissions fees, and events, check out its website at preservationvirginia.org/historic-sites/bacons-castle.

For information about Chippokes State Park admission, cabin rental fees, and events, see the website: www.stateparks.com/chippokes_state_park_in_virginia.html

Smith's Fort Plantation is at 217 Smith Fort Lane, Surry, Virginia 23883. Check their website for admission details and open hours. www.preservationvirginia.org/historic- sites/smiths-fort-plantation/.

Smithfield Packing Company is located at 111 Commerce Street, Smithfield, VA 23430.

To find out more about historic Smithfield, Isle of Wight, and area events, check the Smithfield Visitor's welcome site: https://www.smithfieldva.gov/297/Visitors

Free guided walking tours of Smithfield's historic district are offered throughout the year from the Visitor's Center at 318 Main Street, Smithfield, Virginia 23430.

The Isle of Wright County Museum is at 103 E. Main Street.

The Old Courthouse of 1750 is available any day or time for group tours with prior notice.

Smithfield Station (the restaurant), 415 South Church Street, Smithfield, Virginia 23430.
https://smithfieldstation.com/

Smithfield Inn & William Rand Tavern 112 North Main Street, Smithfield, Virginia 23430.
http://www.smithfieldinn.com

Smithfield Gourmet Bakery and Cafe, 218 Main Street, Smithfield, Virginia 23430
http://smithfieldgourmetbakery.com/

Windsor Castle Park, 301 Jericho Road, Smithfield, VA 23430.
https://www.windsorcastlepark.com/166/About-the-Park

For information about free guided tours of the cemetery check the Isle of Wight County Museum website at www.historicisleofwight.com

Historic Luke's Church and Cemetery is located at 14477 Benns Church Boulevard, Smithfield, Virginia 23430. https://stlukesmuseum.org.

Fort Huger, located at Route 10 at 15080 Talcott Terrace, Isle of Wight County, Virginia. From Route 10, follow the Civil War Trails signage. Open dawn until dusk. http://www.historicisleofwight.com/fort-huger.html

Located at 7410 Fort Boykin Trail, Smithfield, Virginia 23430.
https://www.historicisleofwight.com/fort-boykin.html

Open daily from 8 a.m.-dusk. Fort Boykin is located along the James River in Isle of Wight County.

Boykin's Tavern is located at 17146 Monument Circle, Isle of Wight, Virginia.

http://www.historicisleofwight.com/boykins-tavern.html

Stop for breakfast, lunch and dinner at the Virginia
Diner, 408 County Drive North, Wakefield, Virginia
23888. http://www.vadiner.com.

Riddick's Folly is located at 510 N. Main Street,
Suffolk, Virginia 23434. http://riddicksfolly.org/

Baron's Pub-Suffolk, 185 N Main St, Suffolk, Virginia
23434, https://www.baronspub.com/suffolk

More information about the Cedar Hill Cemetery can
be found at:
www.suffolkva.us/Facilities/Facility/Details/Cedar-Hill-
Cemetery-53

Suffolk Seaboard Station Railroad Museum, 326 North
Main Street, Suffolk, Virginia 23434.
www.suffolktrainstation.com/

You can see when the Legends of Main Street ghost
tour is held, by checking online at
http://www.visitsuffolkva.com/.

Great Dismal Swamp National Wildlife Refuge
(Virginia and North Carolina), 3100 Desert Road,
Suffolk, Virginia.
https://www.fws.gov/refuge/great_dismal_swamp/